D1050776

Loving Richie

Dear Jasmine —
my gift to you
for your gifts to
me & you for
thank you &
inviting me to
join your world &
the
group !!

♡

Suzanne

Credits
"You Rona, You" was originally published under the title, "Frozen in
Time" in the anthology, A Loving Testimony: Remembering Loved Ones
Lost to AIDS, edited by Leslea Newman, Crossing Press, 1992.
"Today is my 38th birthday" first appeared as a poem in the anthology,
Voices of the Grieving Heart, edited by Mike Bernhardt, Cypress Point
Press, 1994.

Copyright © 2008 Suzanne Freed
All rights reserved.
ISBN: 1-4392-0453-5
ISBN-13: 978-1439204535
Library of Congress Control Number: 2008906978

Visit www.amazon.com to order additional copies.

Any clients mentioned are creations of the author and not meant to
resemble any persons living or dead.

SUZANNE FREED

LOVING RICHIE
THE TRUE STORY OF HEARTS CONNECTED BEYOND DEATH

2008

Loving Richie

ACKNOWLEDGEMENTS

My life is so blessed...

To my mother, Missy, now in spirit; and my father, Sol, who is very much alive and well, for their love, support and belief in me.

I take time to remember my grandmother, Mariam, who was the first woman in our family to be a published writer; her poetry and opinion pieces were published in the *Jewish Daily Forward* in the late 1920's and into the 1950's. She emigrated to New York in the 1900's leaving behind her family who all perished in the Holocaust.

For their love, my brother, Joel and Wendy, my sister-in-law, and my two awesome nieces, Nicole and Tracey.

Bruce and Toni, my dear cousins, for their love and belief in me.

Lorraine Blue for her presence through those years.

Mother Meera for opening the door in 1993.

I want to thank Jane Dystel, who long ago, in 1992, signed me on as a client and tried to sell the original version of this book.

Many, many thanks for believing in my writing and the story of Richie and me. Your original interest and belief was a true gift; it kept me moving forward to bring this book to birth.

As Bette Midler sings, "you've got to have friends." I am rich and truly blessed with the love of friends. How to say "thank you" is beyond me.I would need a chapter for each friend.

My dear friends from the years *before* 1986 for your abiding love and holding me up during that dark time; Jan Boddie, Leslie Brooke, Helen Clark, Gail Davido, Cyn Friedman, Beca Kulinovich, Cynthia Pastor, Marlene Ritchie, Barb Silver, Babs, Wendy, Frances.

To those who entered my life years later for your love, support and friendship.
Rochelle Collins, Daya Cramer, Amalia Darling, Wilma Friesema, Kathleena Gorga, Deepti Sanders, Harsha Carley, Vedavati, Cindy Horvath, Felix Lee Lerma, Valerie Lloyd, Rachael Masson, Ted Zeff, Claire Elizabeth Robbat de Sophia.

To my "Solo Improv Sisters": Theresa Dailey, Chris Kammler, Kim McCourt, Carol LaDue, Joanne Sultar, Margaret Thalhuber-for inspiration, laughter,general cheerleading and love; and to Vickie for loving, creative support.

Elaine Bellezza, for your loving friendship and immeasurable help with this book, both emotional and logistical. You read my first draft long ago and believed in the book from that moment on.

Paula McGuire, for segues, laughter, loving friendship, belief in and support for all my creative work.

An enormous thanks to all of my friends and colleagues who over the years have helped me realize my dreams, helped me work through my grief and who have touched me with their love.
I am grateful that there are too many to mention and I hold all of you in my heart though your name may not be in print here.

For inspiration: Oprah Winfrey, Marianne Williamson, Iyanla Vanzant, Whoopie Goldberg, Rachel Remen, Madeline L'Engle, Hildegarde of Bingen, Etty Hillesum, Hilda Charlton, Marianne Woodman, Pema Chodron, Stephen Levine, Jack Kornfeld, Viktor Frankl, Sharon Salzberg, Martha Beck, Julia Cameron; and thousands of books by thousands of authors, both fiction and non-fiction, whose words touched and transformed my life from the day those funny black marks on paper began making sense to me.

Thank you to my amazing and patient Booksurge team: Abdur-Rahim Kelley, Lindsey and Lee Sanderlin.

Loving Richie: The true story of hearts connected beyond death is available on-line through www.amazon.com.

With Great Love I Humbly Offer This Book

At The Lotus Feet

Of My Beloved Guru

Sri Mata Amritanandamayi Devi.

Known To All

As

Amma

A TIME OF INNOCENCE

I remember the night my baby brother was born. He was my birthday gift when I was three years old. Or so I thought. He was born February 19, 1952. Exactly one week, to the day, before my third birthday.

My older brother Joel and I were running around our bedroom, bouncing on the beds and leading Aunt Florry and Uncle Vic on a merry chase. They were staying with us since Mom was in the hospital having a baby. I doubt I understood what "having a baby" meant but the night felt exciting.

My memories of childhood are sketchy but I recall the silent, Kodak-color faded movies that Uncle Vic shot. There we are moving along in that jerky way of 1950 home movies. There is Richie, bundled up in a maroon colored snowsuit, gray muffler tied around his neck, mittens attached to his tiny hands. There I am in a red-colored plaid winter coat, brown velvet hat tied beneath my chin towing Richie along. There's Joel, throwing snowballs, looking bored. Joel was born in 1945 and the many years difference in age from Richie and me put him in his own category of "older brother." As we grew up the age difference mattered more at some times and less, finally, as we entered our adult years.

My favorite home movie is the one of Joel, Mom, Aunt Florry, me and Richie in the dining room. Dad and Uncle Vic are nowhere to be seen because they are behind the camera. We are playing a board game and Richie is in his high chair.

The late autumn sunlight is streaming through the window lighting up his blonde hair and his face as Mom is feeding him. There he sits, a chubby-faced blonde, blue-eyed baby laughing and banging his spoon on his high-chair tabletop. Happy. His nickname is Happy.

YOU RONA, YOU

I was his big sister and fiercely protective. The day my friend
Rona shoved Richie down on the sidewalk was the day my
family saw a side of me that surprised us all. I was six
years old and Rona five. Who knows what caused her angry
outburst at my brother. Next thing I knew I was shoving *her* to
the ground, sitting on her and pummeling her with my fists.

"You Rona, you, don't ever, ever, hurt my brother." It took
both our mothers to pull me off Rona's back. My mom was
angry and astounded but she and Helen, Rona's mom, began
choking back laughter underneath their concern. My mom
knelt before me trying to look strict.

"Suzanne Renee, what are you doing? Apologize to Rona
at once."

"But Mom, she shoved Richie first. I was just protecting
him." Helen turned to Rona who was still sniffling into her
sleeve.

"Rona, did you pick on Richie? You know better than
that, apologize to him right now." Rona mumbled something,
I mumbled something. Richie stopped crying and my mom
gathered us to her in a big hug, including Rona in her embrace.

That night I heard the grown-ups laughing as my mom's
voice rose above their laughter, "*You Rona, you!* It was so sweet
to see how fiercely she defended Richie."

I pulled my two dolls, Cookie and Barbara, close to my
chest, wondering why they thought it all so funny. He was my

baby brother and no one; *no one* was ever going to hurt him, not as long as I was there to protect him.

We grew up in the years of *Wonder Bread* sandwiches, cola syrup you could buy at the soda fountain in the candy store, and bring home to creat your own sodas; a real bakery shop where mom bought freshly baked challah for Friday nights; and pizza parlors that sold slices for twenty-five cents including a soda. There was *Captain Kangaroo,* and *Superman,* on television; milk bottles delivered into little wooden boxes on the front steps, or stoop, of the apartment. There were wooden floors in the A&P market, and the grocery clerk used a wooden "thig-a-muh-jig" to move the next person's groceries closer to him. There were tiny white trucks selling "Good Humor" or "Bungalow Bar" ice-cream whose tinny bells called us into the tree-lined streets in the hot, humid New York summers. On Sundays we watched Ed Sullivan gathered around the small black and white television set. There were Danny Kaye movies for fifty cents on Saturday afternoons at the Century Meadows movie theater. As we grew older we watched *Dobie Gillis* and his friends Zelda and Maynard G. Krebbs, the beatnik, on television. In the afternoons we danced to *American Bandstand* hosted by Dick Clark and endless westerns filled the television screen from *Have Gun, Will Travel* to *Gunsmoke* and *Bonanza.*

The home movies in my mind melt into one long film, skipping through the years. There is Richie, with long hair flopping in his eyes, and me, with my bleached blonde hair streaming down my back. I have Kodak photographs of Richie perched atop the boulders of Central Park looking pensively away from my camera. I remember the day I took that picture. It was Easter Sunday. Fifth Avenue was closed to traffic and people were parading up and down the long street in their Easter best. We joined the strolling crowd and were soon accompanied by someone dressed in a gorilla suit wearing a straw Easter bonnet. There we were, two kids in Navy surplus pea coats, long haired, sporting political buttons on our lapels, strolling down 5th avenue in our version of Sunday best with a gorilla at our side. We wandered into Central Park leaving the parade and our gorilla friend behind. It was warm and sunny; the air alive with the scent of grass, flowers, and that quality which informs you in no uncertain terms that it is, yes, spring.

We clambered up boulders in the park, perching atop the tallest one, gazing at the skyline and the people below us. Central Park was quiet that morning and Richie and I felt close to each other and content. He was 17 years old and I, 20. Life felt exciting, dramatic, and full of possibilities. We felt exciting and dramatic leaning on the rocks, looking up at the trees, and beyond, murmuring about important things, hanging out together without our usual brother-sister friction. 1969 and Easter Sunday in New York City.

Richie shared adventures with me and my friends, Michele, Fran and Cynthia. The four of us became friends in junior high school and were inseparable. Although he was three years younger than us my friends liked him and at times we included him in our trips to Manhattan.

By the time were juniors in high school we began sneaking into Broadway matinees when the doors opened for the intermission after the first act. We saw the second and third acts of show after show. The black-uniformed ushers looked the other way when suddenly they saw these teenagers scattered throughout the theater in seats that had been vacant for Act one. But sometimes we were busted and "shooed" out of the theater laughing and running away as fast as we could.

"Hurry up Suzie, you are just dragging along, run faster before we get arrested." Richie was running backwards urging me on as he laughed, stopping suddenly to light a cigarette and laughing again, watching me leaning on my knees gasping for breath.

"Richie, stop making fun of me. We aren't going to get arrested. We haven't been arrested one time and they really don't care."

I finally reached him and leaned against his shoulder trying to grab his Tareyton cigarette from his lips. "Hey, light your own damn cigarette, moocher!" Laughing again he batted my hand away from his face. I tried to tickle him through his Navy pea coat but he danced away from me.

Many a winter morning after surfacing from the subway Richie and I walked to the Hilton hotel on Avenue of the Americas, or 6th avenue. We took the elevator to the top of the hotel—the Presidential suite floor, walked to the fire exit door, climbed the stairs to the roof of the building and, ignoring the "Do Not Enter" and "Danger" signs, we picked our way among the wires and pipes at our feet; and there she was, the city, stretching out in all her glory, this was many years before taller buildings obstructed the panoramic view. There *we* were, perching on the concrete roof, drinking hot cups of coffee and, of course, smoking our usual cigarettes, breath frosty in the cold winter air; two kids from Queens feeling very much like "outlaws" in our private world of teenage daring.

The other reality was that those years were also angst-filled and difficult. I don't know whose adolescence was more painful, mine or his. I suppose they were equally challenging. Try growing up knowing you are, or might be, oh my God—gay. I would like to blame the pain of it on the fact that we grew up in some tiny, tiny town but we grew up in Bayside Queens, and lived forty-five minutes by subway away from one of the most sophisticated cities in the world. No it wasn't that. It was because growing up different is painful. Growing up in the late 1950's and early 1960's *and* being different was excruciating.

I wandered through my tortured adolescence wishing there was some kind of cure I could undergo to make me attracted to males in the same way I was attracted to females. In the 1960's people were being hauled off for shock treatment for being gay. In 1968 my friend Lisa was forced out of a relationship she was in with a girl. Her girlfriend was forcibly admitted to a mental hospital because her parents found out. Lisa was no longer allowed to see *me* because I knew about their relationship and her parents threatened to tell mine all about it, as if I had been an accomplice to a murder. I will never forget the day her mom called and threatened to tell my parents about what had happened. Her voice reached out across the phone terrifying me.

"You will *never* be allowed to see Lisa again. Don't even try to, because if you do I will call your parents so fast your head will spin." She slammed the phone down and I was left trembling and shaking. That night I told my parents about everything. I didn't want to be afraid of that crazy mother upsetting my parents.

"Lisa was involved with another girl?" Dad's voice squeaked in astonishment, but before he could utter another word Mom jumped in.

"Shh, Sol, can't you see Sue's upset? Are you going to be okay?" She reached out her arms to me as I fell into them, sobbing. I lost my best friend that day because of who she loved and it made no sense at all. I nodded my head as I uttered muffled words against her chest.

"Yeah Mom, I'll be okay, I miss her so much, we've been friends for so many years. Mom, it's just not fair." "No Sue, it's not and if that woman ever calls here again I'll tell her a thing or two." I could only imagine what my mom would say to Lisa's mother, none of it nice.

How was I supposed to feel okay even thinking about my feelings for girls, let alone talking about them to my parents or anyone? I was depressed that entire year. My closest friend had been ripped away from me; how could I feel anything but ashamed and afraid of my feelings for girls when this was the result of loving someone of the same sex?

Richie confided in me his feelings for boys when he was fifteen. I vaguely recall trying to reassure him. I hope I didn't tell him it was a phase he would outgrow. Our textbooks back in the dark ages usually had one paragraph about *it*. These textbooks were used in our "hygiene" classes, "hygiene" being a codeword for sex education back in the late 1950's and early 60's.

The paragraph imparted some homophobic drivel that it was common to feel closer to friends of the same sex in adolescence and that maybe, some people, but really very, very, very few, in fact a teeny, tiny percent, *maybe* felt somewhat attracted to their friends. **BUT- not to worry.** This was only a PHASE you were going through and you would outgrow it soon- in fact you would outgrow it immediately after reading this paragraph if not sooner. So there.

A lot of good this did me. I was different too and I knew it and hated myself for it. I can only assume that Richie was also depressed by his attraction to boys. I know he loved one boy in particular and that they "fooled around". But for boys it was even more difficult. After all, girls could hug and kiss and have sleep over parties, many, many sleepover parties. I remember my torment at those parties. I would lie awake for hours longing for a friend in the next bed and hating myself.

The irony was that Richie was popular with girls throughout junior and high school. In my junior year of high school I blossomed and was popular with the boys. I was president of my illegal high school sorority. I loved dancing and my sense of humor was my biggest asset. No one would have known that beneath my laughter I was miserable and depressed.

There was my kid brother; handsome, great dancer, well-dressed, funny, and smart; ahh, those Frieds, lusting after each other's dates, but who knew? In the 1960's gay or bi-sexual teens did not come out to anyone; coming out to myself and denying it at the same time caused me to alternate between suicidal depression and hopelessness most of my adolescence.

I want to move along and away from those years to the years of our twenties. In order to escape my attraction to women I did the best thing an obedient, twenty-two year old Jewish female could do in 1971, I married. Pushing my feelings for women away from myself I left home the only way I could, by walking down the aisle and into the arms of someone I loved, but was not in love with. Steve was a sweet and loving young man—our marriage lasted two years.

In the meantime Richie and I continued to have our share of ups and downs. We fought, became angry, made up and at times I know I hurt him deeply. At times he hurt me as well. But underneath was the enduring bond of love that nothing could diminish. There were times we did not speak to one another for weeks or months. One of those times was soon after he came out about his sexuality. He arrived home in late August of 1972 after a solo trip to Europe. There he was at

Kennedy Airport, just exiting Customs, beautifully tanned, with an earring in one ear. In New York in 1972, it was not considered trendy for a man to wear an earring. It was startling and it also courted danger. It was a bold statement as a not so subtle nod to other gay men and it made Richie an easy target for those who hated gays. I admired his guts and also worried for his safety.

Richie moved to Manhattan and I didn't visit him for months. It's hard to admit this. For years I carried guilt and sorrow over the way I handled, or didn't handle, his coming out. I was intensely threatened by his coming out. He mirrored all the unasked and ignored questions I had about my sexuality. Here I was hiding in my miserable marriage. I was fighting constantly with Steve. I was drinking to excess, smoking too many cigarettes and eating Alka-Seltzer to quell the slowly growing ulcer in my stomach. The pains were caused by my absolute fury at being married and living a lie. I was miserable and in the closet and my brother had bravely walked through Customs proclaiming his sexuality for all to see.

Months later I entered therapy, knowing I could not continue to live this anguished half-life. I avidly read Anais Nin's journals, which were popular in the early 1970's; her seemingly free-wheeling, sexually open lifestyle only reinforced my conviction to explore my sexuality. I wrote to Nin and she wrote back, encouraging me to follow my longing for freedom.

In February of 1973 I told Steve I had to live alone and explore my feelings for women. I moved out on a rainy, cold Sunday in April. Steve left town to visit his brother in Washington D.C.; the pain of my leaving more then he could bear alone. Joel and I drove my few belongings to Manhattan, into my very own studio apartment on East 85th and York Avenue. I was thrilled to live in the "Big Apple" with my baby brother Richard living only a few blocks away on East 76th near 3rd avenue. I was also terrified because it was the first time in my life living alone; living in my very own apartment in the most exciting city in the world.

ICED COFFEE AFTERNOONS

New York City was an integral part of our lives. I loved the beat and rhythm of the city. I reveled in the cacophony of the taxi horns and the shouts of drivers flinging their middle fingers into the air at whomever crossed their paths, with or without the permission of the traffic lights. I loved walking the miles of New York's streets. People watching was my favorite pastime; seeing the spontaneity of the street theater encounters, window shopping, and feeling that surging energy which *is* New York. But most of all I loved meeting Richie at one of our favorite spots.

The heat of New York in summer stifled me as I strolled along Third Avenue. Smells of rotting dogshit, subway and bus fumes assailed my nostrils. It was summer of 1973 and Richie and I were going to meet for coffee. Meeting for coffee was a New York summer/winter/spring/fall ritual for us. It all depended on our respective states of mind. Meeting for coffee meant long, leisurely talks over hot coffee in winter and iced coffee in summer. I knew summer had officially arrived when I found myself sitting across from my brother with two, tall sweating glasses of iced coffee between us and the inevitable ashtray overflowing with cigarettes and ashes. We met and talked about many things; my divorce, his career plans, my teaching, our family, the latest man he was dating, his dreams, my dreams.

Sometimes we met at the *Third Avenue El*, a coffee shop located close to Bloomingdale's and named for the long-gone section of the IRT subway that had clattered overhead. Or we met at *Daly's Dandelion* on Third Avenue. One night we were there with Michele. Richie and she had become friends when Richie moved out of our parent's home and into *The Grange*, the house Michele and others rented in Flushing.

It was eleven on a weekday night and we had just been seated in the near empty restaurant. The door opened and I gazed up from my menu. There they were. John Lennon and Yoko Ono. Walking into Daly's, sitting down at a table. I grabbed Michele's arm in a death grip and whispered, "Don't look but John Lennon and Yoko have just walked in. Don't look!"

She responded to me with wariness from years of my playing "make you look" games.

"You're kidding right, I hate when you do that Suzanne, it's so immature." Michele had fallen victim many times to my "don't look now but there's Katherine Hepburn or Greta Garbo" ploys. Both these legends lived in New York City and Michele and Fran and I spent many hours strolling through their neighborhoods in the hope of encountering them.

When we were depressed we made pilgrimages to Greta Garbo's apartment building on Sutton place, off the East River, and stood for hours gazing longingly up at her building's windows hoping to catch a glimpse of the mystery woman. The doorman would good-naturedly shoo us along but we always came back. He had a bulge underneath his arm that his long doorman's coat only accentuated and we teased him about it.

"Why do you need a gun? We aren't going to hurt Garbo. We only want to go upstairs and pay homage to her." We giggled and lit up our Tareyton cigarettes trying to appear sophisticated.

He laughed and replied, "You lasses don't have a snowball's chance in Hell of gaining entry to the building. So please move your pretty selves across the street, now there's a bunch of good girls."

He had a delightful Irish brogue and made us feel important enough to warrant his attention. It was a ritual we followed at least once a month. It cheered us up to be so close to greatness and we admired her reported solitude. She was someone to admire as an artist and as an independent woman who needed no one; or so we thought. Like all star worship it was based on conjecture, all smoke and mirrors. I thought about all this as I whispered to her again,

"Michele. I am serious this time. Okay, turn around slowly. Look."

Richie looked up from his menu. Then he leaned towards Michele and said, "It's true Michele, they are here, it is them." His voice was pitched low and there was an urgent command to it. Since Richie never played silly "made you look" games Michele believed him.

We tried to be subtle as we turned to look at them. What were they eating? They were engrossed in conversation. Never one to be shy I decided to go to the restroom, which was only accessible by passing their table. I studiously avoided staring at them as I walked past. After what seemed an appropriate amount of time I re-emerged and walked back to report from my foray to the restroom.

"Cheesecake!" I crowed triumphantly. "They are eating cheesecake." I delivered this news as if it was unusual. Daly's was famous for its cheesecake but to know that Lennon and Ono were eating it made it somehow exotic and newsworthy. Michele ran to the phone booth in the back of the restaurant to call her two brothers and tell them that at this very moment we were witnessing history being made. Richie was cool. He didn't get up to use the restroom in order to spy on them. He wasn't giggling nervously. He just sat there eating his cheesecake. He was not overly impressed, or so it appeared. On our way out the door we all smiled at John and Yoko, smiled as only New Yorkers can when they meet celebrities on the street. It is a casual smile, like "I know who you are but I am not going to disturb your privacy." They smiled back at us.

As soon as we were out of view of Daly's, Michele and I grabbed hands and jumped up and down. Richie stood there grinning at us like an amused parent. But I knew he was excited. He saved a napkin which had fallen off the famous couple's table as we walked out. He waved it at us and tucked it into his jacket pocket.

There were times I met Richie at the *Whitney Museum* on Madison Avenue and 75th to look at our favorite exhibit, the permanent Calder Circus; we loved Calder's whimsy and playfulness—it was one more thing we shared. Downstairs was the museum's café where we had iced coffee and rice pudding. Richie talked about traveling to Europe again, about his writing and his dreams. We talked about our favorite poets, our love lives, our work, all the while our hands grabbing for one another in affection, our fingers cold from the icy glasses.

No time apart can ever tarnish these precious memories. It all lay before us, our dreams, our heartbreaks, our lives. Summertime in New York, the city shimmering in the heat and Suzie and Richie sipping iced coffee, forever.

WEST COAST DREAMS

Time remains frozen only in our memories. In April of 1978 Richie moved to L.A. to pursue his writing dreams and in June I moved to San Francisco. I was burnt out from teaching in the N.Y.C. school system and also wanted to live in a city that was gay friendly. I had fallen in love with San Francisco on a visit in 1974. The thought of living on the West coast with Richie living an hour plane ride away helped me feel less alone. It was reminiscent of my move to New York City in 1973; I seemed to always follow in his footsteps.

The 1980's unfolded in a blur of dating, dancing, and drinking too much. I flew to L.A. to visit Richie and he flew to San Francisco to hang out with me and explore the gay scene. My visits to Richie were mixed. We'd have at least one argument, make-up soon after and then go shopping. Unfortunately I inherited my mom's attitude about shopping; get there when the doors open, on a weekday if possible, run in, find what you want, no dawdling, try it on, buy it or not, then leave.

But Richie loved shopping as did our father and our older brother. Maybe it was just a "Fried male thing". Richie and I spent time strolling through the Beverly Center, he'd grab my hand, hold it for a moment, then pull me into a store to admire some shirt or jacket he'd spotted.

"Hey Suzie, what do you think about this? Does it make me look fat?"

I snorted, "Richie, the word fat and you in clothing of any style never crosses my mind. You look very stylish in it, tres chic." I said this in my really poor French accent. He made a face at me, "Well I don't have the money to buy it now, maybe next paycheck," and pulling my arm to get me moving, we wandered the mall until the next fabulous item of clothing drew his attention.

Saturday nights we had dinner, usually sushi, with his friend Tommy. In later years, after Tommy moved to New York, his friend Joey joined us. Sundays were the time for late, late brunch and taking me to the airport for my trip home. Inevitably we argued the day I was leaving, it was too much for us, the loneliness of saying good bye, the distance from each other; and the difference in our lifestyles was always grist for the brother—sister mill of arguing. His favorite argument was a critique of my "wasted youth".

"Suzie, why don't you just take yourself seriously? You're so talented and you are just wasting your life, drinking, dating a million women-" I harrumphed at him. My blue eyes glaring into his blue eyes. "Well, okay, not a million women, but really- why aren't you writing more or doing something aside from working at that stupid bookstore?"

"Richie for one time can we please not argue about my life, look at your own life and leave me out of your endless criticizing." Stony silence fell between us. By the time he dropped me at the airport we hugged and kissed as if nothing had happened. It was often this way with Richie seeing my great potential and my resisting his vision of my life; but there was always fun and laughter woven between the fighting and sniping.

RICHIE, TOMMY AND SHOES

My brother and his best friend Tommy had strange ideas about meeting men. Tommy and Richie were inseparable until Tommy moved to New York City. Each of them had a zany sense of humor and the same outlook on life, slightly tilted. Fashion was important but shoes really made the man. In fact no man could be "made" or met, unless he had the right look. Ahh, the shallowness of youth. Tommy would very solemnly say to me,

"Suzie, you can judge a man by his shoes. Richie and I will go out and before we even look at faces we look at the floor. Shoes, that's where it's at, some guys look so together and wonderful but when you look down, what's on their feet? Ugh, scruffy moccasins with holes in them, or ugly, unpolished wing tips. Or some beat up pair of topsiders that you know they love more than life itself and you know they have ten more pairs just like them in their closet at home. Shoes Suzie, SHOES are the best way to pick a man." Then he winked at me and smiled and I wondered if he was having a joke at my expense or really letting me on a secret code that the two of them lived by—at least in their world of cruising in bars.

By the end of Tommy's discourse there was Richie drinks in hand. He looked at Tommy laughing and smiling. "Are you telling her about that shoe thing, *again?*"

I can see the three of us standing alongside the bar looking at the floor and discussing the various shoes that moved past us in an endless parade. I don't recall if either of them met anyone that night but I had the distinct sense that this must be what a salesperson at Gucci's felt like.

Fashion was important to Richie. If my feet were killing me from my latest pair of heels he smilingly reminded me that if it didn't hurt it wasn't worth the look. Then, smiling innocently he'd lightly slap my back. One year he wrote a few columns for the *L.A. Times* fashion section. His favorite piece was on the new trend in bow ties. The fashion editor didn't run it and told him he was wrong about the trend. Was this guy humbled when *Women's Wear Daily* carried a piece about the *same* designer's bowties a week *after* Richie's column was to run. What would have been a scoop for the *Times* turned into nothing. Those ties became "the rage" in the late 1980's. I wonder if the fashion editor ever apologized to my trend-spotting brother.

Both my brothers could spot a fashion trend ahead of others. I bought my first pair of bell-bottom jeans when Joel took me to a store in Greenwich Village, The Brick Shed House, in 1966. The pants were railroad stripe and I loved them. That was the last time I was a trend setter and it was only because Joel encouraged me to buy them. Richie was wearing scarves around his forehead in the discos long before John Travolta split his pants on the silver screen, and he began dressing in layers before I knew that layers were not just part of birthday cakes.

FORESHADOWING

In November 1981 Richie called to ask me if I would fly to L.A. the following weekend. He was having a biopsy. My voice was shaking as I responded in shock, "A biopsy? What for?"

There was a momentary silence. "My doctor wants to rule out this "gay cancer" thing, my lymph nodes are really swollen."

"Gay cancer? I remember reading something about that in the local gay newspaper, what the hell is going on?"

"No one seems to know. Anyway can you come down? The procedure is Friday." "Of course I'll come. I'll tell my managers at the bookstore I need the day off. How are you? Do you want me to come down this weekend? I can you know."

He thought for a moment and then said in a quiet, scared voice, "I think I'd like to visit San Francisco, why don't I come up there?"

"Great, let me know what flight you'll be on. I can meet you at the airporter bus station."

"No. I'll take a cab from the airport to your place. I'll fly in tomorrow. Talk to you soon. I love you Suzie."

"I love you too Richie."

He hated when I called him Richie, preferring I call him Richard. It often slipped out when I wasn't thinking. It was striking to me that this time he didn't chide me for using that name from our childhood. I stood there in the late afternoon sunlight looking at the garden outside my studio apartment. I was stunned. I was terrified. Cancer? My baby brother? No way. NO way.

Friday afternoon found me smoking too many cigarettes and drinking too many cups of coffee. Richie was on his way from the airport.

When he arrived at my apartment door I gathered him to me and held him for a long time. Finally he pushed me away, "Hey, let me in the door first, my duffel bag is getting smooshed."

" Well I couldn't wait to hug you!"

We decided he's stay with my friend Marlene the next night and with me for Friday night. My studio had a single bed and a tiny futon couch, not the best situation for privacy. Finding a sushi restaurant was the next order of business.

"Hey Richard, what about eating in Japantown? There's a great place there you'll love it?" His teasing never ceased. "Well your taste in sushi isn't as gourmand as mine-"

"Ugh you are such a sushi snob. Let's just go eat tuna melts somewhere, that's a kind of cooked sushi, on rye." We loved tuna melts and fries, it was a comfort food that we shared and I could eat them all the time. He shrugged at me as he responded, "Funny, very funny, nope let's go to Japantown, if I hate it you can pay the bill."

We ordered huge amounts of sushi and the sake flowed, well Richie drank more than I did because I knew I couldn't go dancing if I drank too much; being able to stand upright was a requirement when I went dancing.

The weekend was a blur of eating out, dancing in the bars on Castro street, and finally, on Saturday night, we parted at midnight; Richie went on to Trocadero's, a well-known bar that had beautiful male fan dancers in the corners of the dance floor and a stage, where Sylvester, one of the stars of the disco world, often performed.

Sunday we met in the Castro for brunch, drinking the requisite Bloody Mary's along with our food. A few hours later we hailed a cab and Richie left for the airport. That night we talked on the phone. I was alone in my studio, with my Franklin stove's wood fire crackling away.

"Richie, just try not to worry too much, I know that's easy for me to say but try not to be too crazy."

A long sigh answered me and then Richie's voice, very quietly, came over the phone, "Suzie I am so scared. What if I'm sick? All these night sweats and chills, and my swollen glands under my arms, God I wish Friday was over already."

Helpless to know what to say I repeated myself.

"Richie, you're going to be fine. It's good the doctor wants to be safe and see what's going on, you're okay. Call me anytime, day or night, anytime at work."

I flew to L.A. Thursday night. We left for the hospital in the dark at five in the morning. It was an outpatient procedure but it took hours until they rolled him into the operating room. I sat in the waiting room, smoking too many cigarettes and having long distance talks with Mom and Dad.

Finally a very tired looking doctor walked into the waiting room and came towards me extending his hand. "Hello Suzanne, I'm Dr. Parker."

"Hi Doctor. How is he?"

"He's a bit groggy but fine. The biopsy is negative."

I began crying with relief.

"Can I go get him?"

"Certainly. Take him home. He's cranky and hungry, so take good care of him."

"I will" I shook the doctor's hand and rushed off to Richie.

We had our first argument in the room.

"No. I won't use the wheelchair and I won't sit in the wheelchair. I don't need a wheelchair."

"Richard it's the hospital rules…"

"Fuck those."

The nurse appeared just then and he grudgingly sat in the wheelchair holding tightly to the stuffed toy football player I had bought to cheer him up.

Our next argument came at the car. He turned and looked at me with determination in his eyes.

"Give me the keys. I'll drive." He held out his hand gesturing towards the keys.

I answered him in my older sister knows best voice. "Richard you're still uncomfortable from the surgery and probably a bit groggy."

Without another word he grabbed the keys out of my hand and opened the door. I walked around the car and sat inside in silence. Looking back I realize that it was his way to assert some control over an experience totally out of his control.

Back at his apartment he crawled into bed and fell asleep instantly. I ordered pizza for dinner and a few of his friends dropped by. When he woke up we sat in his bedroom watching the movie, "Flashdance" on television. He was exhausted and stayed in bed all day Saturday. Sunday we went out for brunch and life went back to normal.

At least I wanted to think that it did. I flew home to San Francisco that Sunday evening. Later when I was home I wept. I wept from the fear that sat in my heart and the fear I saw in my brother's eyes. I wept because I had to be the "big" sister and take care of my baby brother and I didn't really know what that meant.

Nothing went back to normal. Richie was battling endless symptoms of what was later labeled "ARC", or A.I.D.S. Related Complex. Night sweats, sore throats, extreme fatigue, chills, swollen lymph nodes, thrush, and herpes, which, years later, invaded his esophagus and mouth.

We didn't talk about "it" again, but when I packed his home in 1986 I found a copy of a gay paper, *The New York Native*; it's headline screamed in large, bold print: "Mysterious Gay Cancer Baffling Doctors on Both Coasts."

In 1981 no one had died that *we* knew and none of us had a clue about what was silently moving through our world and planting itself like mines in a battlefield.

Richie refused to discuss the biopsy or anything related to his health with me and I shrank back into a state of complete and utter denial. No one I knew was dying so it was not going to happen in my world. Was it?

Life moved on. Richie was climbing his way up the ladder of success. He wrote ad copy for Marantz stereo creating their "Solid Gold" concept. He moved on from Marantz to Fermodyl beauty products but left them when they moved to the Bay area from L.A. In 1982 he landed an interview through a headhunter for Walt Disney Studios.

Richie had a wonderful track record in his field and was gaining notice and winning awards; his work had not gone unnoticed by an industry always seeking outstanding creative talent.

"Suzie what if they find out I'm Jewish and gay?"

"Richie, Walt is dead, the studio is no longer living in

the 1950's, I 'm sure they must have Jewish employees and gay people- Richie, it's HOLLYWOOD. Don't worry you will wow them with who you are, they already know about your talent and they'll love you!"

Of course he was hired and began his career at Disney Studios. The studio was now being run by Michael Eisner and Jeffrey Katzenberg. Richie's boss, Ben Tenn, was Jewish, what more could he ask for?

By 1985 Richie was Director of Disney Home Video Marketing. The industry was in its baby stages and movies on video were slowly becoming part of the world's at home entertainment. Richie invented the concept of *limited release* of the old Disney cartoons on VHS which, after a brief sale time, were then placed back into the vault.

He was winning awards in his industry and was interviewed on *The Today Show* by Jane Pauley. Under Richie's direction, Disney produced an award-winning video, *Too Smart for Strangers*, using Winnie-the-Pooh characters to teach young children to say "no" to strangers. The video was released in partnership with Adam Walsh from the *Missing Children's Foundation.*

But underneath all this success a deadly virus was destroying his immune system. He was increasingly tired; his long trips to Europe promoting Disney, his frequent cross-country trips to New York for business, all were taking a toll on his health and on his emotional well-being.

OF BIRTHDAYS, DISNEYLAND AND SHOCK

February 1986

O n Valentine's Day morning Richie called. His voice sounded incredibly sad. I had never heard him like this, not even the day he called to ask me to come to L.A. for his biopsy.

I gently asked him, "What's wrong honey, Richie, what's going on?"

"Nothing, I just wish you were here."

"You sound so lonely. I'll be coming down in a few weeks; do you want to come up this weekend?" There was silence as he considered my request. Then a big sigh blew over the phone into my ear.

"Nope, I'll stay home; I'm too depressed and tired to fly up. I hope you and Sarah have a fun Valentine's Day." I called him many times that weekend. I was scared to hear him sounding so forlorn and lonely. Celebrating my second Valentine's Day with Sarah brought me little joy—my worry surrounded us like a dark cloud.

On Friday February 21 Sarah and I drove to L.A. The plans were to go to Disneyland with Richie on Saturday. He had invited a few friends out to dinner for his birthday on February 19 and we were going to continue the celebration for both our birthdays that weekend. Richie's secretary Pat met us outside his condominium and gave us keys and the passes to Disneyland. We joked with her about how he hated the theme park but was willing to go because of Sarah and me. I had never been to Disneyland but Sarah had visited many times as a child. I was looking forward to dragging her and Richie on all the rides and seeing Mickey and Minnie strolling around the park.

We decorated Richie's living room with silver and turquoise balloons and streamers and birthday signs. Richie walked into the apartment at 6 p.m. looking distraught. His tie hung from his hand and his shirt was disheveled. I was stunned by how he looked but I plowed ahead and introduced him to Sarah. After barely acknowledging her he went into his bedroom. I looked at her in dismay and shrugged my shoulders.

Just then he called me.

"Suzie, can I see you in here, please?"

I looked at her again and shrugging my shoulders one more time went into his room.

He was standing by his bed.

"Close the door please"

Suddenly feeling very scared I closed the door and sat on the bed.

"Richie, what's wrong?"

"I was at the doctor's. Here, read this."

He thrust a crumpled paper at me. Feeling frightened I moved away from his hand.

"What is it? What?"

Richie waved it at me, his voice pleading, "Read it, please, just read it."

It was a lab report. Two words leapt out at me. *Kaposi sarcoma*. The words began to blur as tears filled my eyes. The lesion on the left arm above the elbow and close to his shoulder was Kaposi's sarcoma. I read it again.

Men with K.S. suffered from disfiguring lesions on their bodies, their faces and worst of all, the lesions attacked their organs. It was a death sentence. It was one of the virulent diseases that struck men with AIDS. There was no treatment for it. Nothing.

"Richie?" I began to cry.

He stared at me for the longest moment.

"Suzie, I have AIDS. What am I going to do?"

I stood up and put my arms around him, holding him as he wept. I held onto him and thought to myself—"My God, no, no, no, not Richie, no, not this, oh God what are we going to do?"

I don't know how long we stood there. Finally I left him so he could shower and change his clothing.

I walked into the living room and sat next to Sarah on the sofa. I stared at her and began to explain what had just happened in his bedroom.

"Sarah, Richie, Richie has..." I began crying again.

"I know Suzie, I know, I heard..."

All my plans for Richie and Sarah and I having fun together and for the two of them to have time getting to know each other fell away

But then I said one of the stupidest things—which proved I was in shock.

"What about Disneyland?"

Her eyes widened in surprise

"Look, let's get through this evening first, is Richie hungry? I saw chicken in the fridge, I'll cook dinner."

He emerged from his room and wordlessly Sarah stood up and hugged him long and hard. In that moment, as I watched her holding him, I felt as though I loved her more than I ever loved anyone.

That night the three of us slept together. Richie crawled in on my side of the guest bed and I held him until close to dawn. There we were—three scared kids in a bed, only there was no mommy and daddy to make us safe. There was nothing to keep us from the nightmare and make the bogey man go away. The bogey man was here to stay.

Richie finished the morning in his bedroom. He called to me from his room when he woke up. "Suzie, I don't want to die. I never wrote my book. I haven't had a live-in relationship, there's so much I want to do with my life, so many plans—" "Richie, you will write your book, you will do all those things. you won't die, not now, you won't..."

I was lying and we both knew it. Five years after his biopsy everything had changed; it was no longer being called the "gay cancer" but AIDS, and we didn't know anyone who survived very long after diagnosis.

Bobby Campbell, a former Olympic gold medalist, was making headlines in San Francisco because he was alive over four years post-diagnosis. But there was no medical reason for his seeming longevity. With no drugs to combat the many opportunistic infections that assaulted people with AIDS, and no money forthcoming from a mute and uncaring Congress, 1986 was an era of little hope and overwhelming despair and death.

I had attended three funerals by now and Richie was hearing of friends on both coasts who were dying. Here I was reassuring him that he would write his novel and have his longed for relationship. What else could I say? I was trying to reassure myself as well as Richie, but the words sounded hollow and false to my ears. What hope was there? What future for my brother? Who was I kidding?

We went shopping on Melrose Avenue later that day. Every few hours I would say, like a mantra, "Well, what about Disneyland? Maybe it will cheer us up?" Finally Richie looked at me in complete exasperation. He pulled me into a doorway, away from the crowds walking by. " Suzanne! I have been diagnosed with AIDS and you want to go to Disneyland? I hate that place on a good day. Are you nuts? I don't want to go to Disneyland. I already feel like I'm on a really awful ride in some lousy movie whose script I didn't write. FUCK Disneyland!"

I nodded mutely. I was so lost. I didn't know what to say to comfort him. The thought of going to Disneyland seemed like heaven compared to all this wandering aimlessly up and down Melrose; isn't denial strange? As if being in Disneyland would be make any difference to what he was going through. In one store Richie purchased a pin that said "NOT ME". He put the pin on and never removed it from his favorite jacket.

We drove to "I Love Juicy's", a health food café. Richie ordered three wheat grass juices to go with our food. After one swallow I made a face:

"Yuck! This tastes like grass. I'm not going to drink anymore of it."

"Suzie this is good for you. A lot of men who are sick are drinking this, it's supposed to help build up the blood."

"Yeah? Well it sure tastes lousy."

"Drink it down."

He could be very bossy in the best of times. This was the worst of times and I obeyed to avoid upsetting him further, and so the weekend stumbled on.

That night Richie invited his friend Fontelle Slater to join us for dinner at his home.

Fontelle worked with Richie at Disney and was his wise, older woman, hippie friend. He teased her about how she dressed but there was also much love for her even in his teasing.

After dinner Richie took her onto the deck overlooking Silverlake Reservoir and told her about his diagnosis. She was too stunned to talk and left soon after.

On Sunday night we talked about Sarah and me staying a few more days. We called our respective workplaces and told them we would not be in due to a family emergency.

I called my manager, Susan, at *Max's Diner* on Folsom and Third Street in San Francisco. I sat on the floor in the bathroom off the guest bedroom. The door was closed. I didn't want Richie to hear me.

I worked lunch shifts five days a week at Max's. We wore poodle skirts, white sneakers and bobby socks. The diner was a fun environment to work in and the hours fit my schedule. I was studying to become a licensed psychotherapist at J.F.K.University and had recently begun my internship seeing clients; waiting tables gave me the money I needed to live on and the flexible hours I needed at the counseling center.

"Hi Susan, it's me, Suzanne." Her voice sounded less than happy to hear from me.

"What's up Suzanne?"

"I'm still in L.A. I'll be staying here until Wednesday. Richie needs me. He was diagnosed with AIDS on Friday and our brother Joel is flying out from the East coast but I want to stay here with Richie until Joel arrives..." There was a moment of stunned silence and then Susan's voice came over the line filled with sadness.

"Oh God, Suzanne, I am so sorry, so very sorry. Of course it's fine to stay there, if there is anything we can do, please let me know."

"Susan, thanks, thanks."

I was crying and could barely speak. I hung up the phone promising to be there on Thursday morning for my shift. The bathroom walls closed around me as I sat weeping into a towel. I felt trapped in a nightmare. I felt hopeless, helpless and so very, very scared. What was going to happen next?

The awful thing about looking back is I see the places where I didn't do it perfectly. Over and over again my therapist, Lorraine, would tell me this was not a Hollywood movie, Richie and I had a real brother sister relationship. I know she was trying to make me see that I could not do this perfectly and that I was doing the best I could. Yes, we were going to fight and be angry with each other; and make up; and fight some more and I could only do so much. She was right; it was not a movie, if it were it would have been billed as a horror film.

That Monday Sarah and I accompanied Richie to work. A commercial shoot was in progress at an ad agency. Disney was promoting the release of *Alice in Wonderland* in video. There was Alice, the Mad Hatter, and Rabbit with his oversized watch, and Dormouse all seated around a huge table set up for the famous tea party.

It was amazingly surreal to see all this come to life. Sarah was intrigued by the filming but I was lost inside myself, detachedly watching Richie doing what he loved best, being with his staff and the crew from the ad agency. What was more surreal was that no one could guess what the weekend had been like. No one knew what terrible secret Richie carried. It was business as usual with my charming and talented brother at the helm of his ship of work and there was no other place he loved to be, bringing to it so much passion and enthusiasm.

At lunchtime we ate sushi and the sake flowed. I welcomed

the buzz and numbness the warm wine brought me. If it were possible I would have crawled into the bottle and stayed there. "Please God," I prayed, "please give me something to numb this pain, anything to numb this pain, please." But God had other plans for Her daughter and drinking myself into oblivion was not one of them.

Sarah and I left L.A. and drove back to San Francisco on Wednesday. Richie begged me to stay until Joel arrived on Thursday. I am ashamed to write this but in January I planned my birthday party for that Wednesday evening. How I wish I had cancelled my party. I was overwhelmed and in shock. The thought of calling all those people and explaining why I had to stay in L.A., or creating a lie to explain it, felt unbearable and maybe in hindsight I can acknowledge how terrified I was. Perhaps I just wanted to run far, far away.

Joey and Mark arrived to stay with Richie as Sarah and I waved goodbye from her car. Back in San Francisco I was not present at my party. Richie had asked me not to tell anyone about his diagnosis and my lips were sealed. My body was there but I was gone. Everyone noticed how strange I seemed. My heart and thoughts were in Los Angeles with Richie. How stupid of me—what was I doing at this party trying to celebrate my birthday. Celebrate? What was there to celebrate? My baby brother had AIDS. Celebrate? Celebrate what?

Joel flew out to be with Richie the following day. I was relieved that he had his big brother with him and it soothed some of my guilty feelings.

ROLLERCOASTER TO HELL

Four weeks later Richie was hospitalized with PCP, or pneumocystic pneumonia. Joel called to tell me the horrible news and I did not fly down there that evening. Why did I wait? I was terrified that my brother was going to die. In 1986 PCP was a death sentence for many men. I was so scared. I didn't' want to see Richie ill, perhaps dying. This was my baby brother. How could I cope with this?

It has taken me a very long time to forgive myself for who I was then and how my fear paralyzed me. I flew to Los Angeles the next day after a long and sleepless night. I walked into his room, he woke up and reached out to me, I leaned over and hugged him. I hated what he looked like; so thin and vulnerable with an oxygen mask on his face. The treatment for PCP was Pentamanidine, a drug that was dripped by I.V. over a four hour period and it had awful side-effects.

In addition to that, PCP was notorious for wasting bodies—Richie lost twenty pounds that week. I visited him every day and drove home to his quiet apartment late each night. I watched him sleep and read trashy romance novels to while away my time.

Sometimes I visited the other men on the "immune-suppressed" ward of Sherman Oaks Hospital, making the rounds, asking if anyone wanted an ice-cream soda or a burger from the outside world. Most of the men smiled wanly at me and whispered "no."

I was lonely and frightened. Nothing had ever prepared me for this. Not one thing in my life prepared me for the possibility that I might become a caretaker to my brother at this young stage in our lives—or at any stage. All our grandparents had passed away by 1980 and although I was sad and missed each of them, their deaths fit more easily into my idea of what the "natural order" of life was supposed to be.

I was flailing about in deep, deep water alongside Richie and I had no life preserver to throw to keep him afloat.

Joel arrived in L.A. the second week of Richie's illness and I flew home for some respite. A week later I flew back and brought him home. He had been in the hospital three weeks. He was so weak and thin. He shuffled like an old, old man into his apartment and went straight to bed. I wanted to go out on the deck and scream and scream. Instead I sat in his room until he fell asleep and finally I took a nap on the couch. I cooked dinner for us and he forced himself to eat.

"I want to gain back all my weight and more, what if I get sick again? I don't want to look like all those men wasting away to skin and bones." He was so proud of gaining each pound. I drove each day to McDonald's to buy him vanilla shakes which he called his medicine as he slurped them down. Each pound gained was a triumph for him over the helplessness he felt.

AIDS is merciless. Just when you think you are on the road to recovery something else slams you down. Richie's denial, like mine, was shattered. This was the battle for his life. Each pound, each day feeling better was a gift. But so much terror surrounded him about the unknown that the gift of each day was sometimes lost in the maelstrom of fear. I carried silent screams inside of myself—all the time.

It was now early April. The roller coaster ride that Richie was on began February 20. It was as if his body knew that he was now officially diagnosed and all hell broke loose. He had fought the ARC symptoms for more than two years and he was weary. The diagnosis was the beginning of the end. After the bout with PCP other crises followed in quick succession. Shock was giving way to numbing acceptance that this was the way it was going to be forever—whatever forever meant.

When I returned to San Francisco I called him daily. He was profoundly depressed because he could not go to work. Losing his work was the blow which shattered his fragile immune system and brought him to his knees in despair. Without his work, his career, he felt he was no one and had nothing. His despair reflected the times we lived in. In 1986 AIDS was a disease of utter and total hopelessness. There were few drugs available to stop the various opportunistic infections that were killing people with AIDS.

The drug, AZT, the first drug used to slow down the virus, was not yet available and was undergoing clinical trials at the labs at UCLA medical hospital. Even his doctor, Joel Parker, a well-known and highly respected physician with a practice filled with men with AIDS, could not get Richie into the clinical trials; Richie was too ill. He had been living with ARC for years while maintaining a high- pressure, relentless work schedule as he climbed the ladder to increasingly more successes at Disney Studios in the fledgling Home Video department and industry.

SHANTI AND ME

My world was crumbling differently than Richie's. My baby brother had AIDS, Acquired Immunity Deficiency Syndrome; that acronym was the ugliest four letter word I knew. I had been a Shanti counselor for one year before Richie became ill. Shanti means peace in Sanskrit. In San Francisco, Charles Garfield created the organization in the 1970's to work with people dying from cancer. When the epidemic of AIDS began he changed its mission to one of working with people with AIDS.

I was drawn, albeit, unconsciously, to working in this arena. At J.F.K.University I enrolled in a class on death and dying. I read Kubler- Ross' book, *Death and Dying*. I read Stephen Levine's *Conversations at the Edge*, a chronicle of his work with his wife, Ondrea, helping the dying. Unwittingly I was preparing for the next chapter in my life. I thought I wanted to be a therapist working with death and dying. When I heard about the Shanti Project I felt I had found the perfect place to begin my training. The amount of denial I was living in is easy to measure in looking back. My denial was so strong I didn't even consider the possibility of my brother becoming a person with AIDS.

Our focus as Shanti volunteers was on supporting people who were dying. With no drugs to combat the myriad diseases that a beleaguered immune system succumbed to death followed swiftly for the majority of newly diagnosed people.

I attended a rigorous 40 hour training over two weekends to become a Shanti counselor. Some people became physical support volunteers: they cooked, cleaned and grocery shopped for clients.

I was an emotional support counselor. I had two clients within weeks of being trained. One client was Daniel, he was twenty-three, a photographer, and we spent our time looking at his portfolio and planning photo shoots for the future; when he felt well we took walks around his neighborhood in Nob Hill with both our cameras at the ready.

My other client was Adam, a man whose lover of six years, was dying. I was Adam's support person as he coped with the enormity of his losing his best friend and life partner. I had all this training and insight into how to work with my clients but I was ill-prepared to deal with the fear, denial, depression, rage, guilt and grief I was experiencing as both a caregiver and a sister.

Daniel was admitted to San Francisco General Hospital with pneumocystic pneumonia. I visited him, held him as he wept on my shoulder, talked with him and his favorite teddy bear; two weeks after he came home from the hospital Richie was diagnosed.

It was more than I could bear. It was impossible for me to wear both hats. My place was with Richie. Feeling both relief and regret I passed my two clients on to another counselor. I said my goodbyes to these two men I had grown very fond of. I simply was in no position to accompany them further on their journeys. My journey with Richie was all that mattered and all I could barely manage.

Richie hated the fact that I was a Shanti counselor. In June of 1985 he lost a good friend who lived in Chicago. When I arrived for a visit on July 4th weekend I was wearing my

Shanti t-shirt. He pointedly asked me not to wear it during my stay with him. I was such an insensitive jerk back then. I wore the t-shirt one afternoon totally disregarding Richie's request. "I asked you not to wear that damn t-shirt. God, Suzie, you are a pain in the ass."

"That's too bad, I like my shirt and I'm proud to be a volunteer. What difference does it make to you?" He shrugged and turned away.

I wish I could go back in time and shake some sense into that woman, for her stunning insensitivity and self-absorption. I have a photograph of the two of us, glowing with sunburns from a day at the Santa Monica boardwalk. We're seated on his new grey loveseat with our arms around each other, him in white, and me in my purple Shanti shirt. There we are smiling at Joey behind the camera; we seem to be blissfully unaware of what was lurking around the corner, reaching out for my brother, waiting to smash into our world and change our lives forever. Denial is such a funny mechanism. It protects and cocoons us from the realities we are not ready to face, but once shattered all that has been kept at bay floods into our lives and psyches with a vengeance.

PARENTS

On September 13, 1985 our mother suffered a major heart attack while she and Dad were visiting me in San Francisco. The heart attack destroyed approximately 80% of her heart muscle. Much of her strength was gone and would never return. The damage to her heart radically altered her life. She was transformed from an active independent woman to someone with an enormously restricted life.

The next day Richie flew in from L.A. and Joel flew in from the East coast. We gathered in Mom's hospital room. She was so pale and looked so small in the bed. She was almost as white as the sheets surrounding her. Richie and I went outside for some air. We sat on a wall outside the hospital. He seemed distant and "off."

"Are you okay Richie? Is something bothering you in addition to Mom's heart attack?" He shrugged and looked away. "No Suzie, I'm fine. Just tired from traveling for work this week. I stopped smoking cigarettes. That's exhausting me too."

Looking back I now know he was lying. He had discovered a lesion on his arm that week but did not confide in me or Joel. He chose to keep the discovery of this lesion to himself until February when he went for the biopsy—days before his 34th birthday. We wandered to other topics of conversation and I did not ask him again about how unusually remote he seemed. He would tell me when and if he was ready. Five months later his secret was no longer a secret and his descent into hell began.

My parents stayed for one month in my apartment in Noe Valley. Mom flew home looking wan and emaciated. Unknown to all of us she was in heart failure; the doctor who took care of her when she was released from St. Francis hospital had neglected to give her the correct medication to help her heart pump and prevent fluid building up in her lungs; when her plane landed at La Guardia airport she was rushed by ambulance to Long Island Jewish hospital for yet another long stay. From the brink death my mother pulled through. For months I talked about suing the doctor for his malpractice; his carelessness and lack of correct diagnosis and treatment. My parents refused to pursue it and perhaps they were right. I cannot imagine what it would have been like if they were immersed in a lawsuit just as Richie was being diagnosed.

In February Richie had sworn Joel and me to secrecy about his diagnosis. He wanted to fly to New York and break the news to our parents in person. Then in early March, barely three weeks after the diagnosis of KS he fell critically ill with PCP and was placed on the critical list at Sherman Oaks Hospital. It was time to tell our parents.

Joel met Dad in Manhattan for lunch. Wendy, Joel's wife, and I were in constant contact—praying all would go as well as could be expected. Poor Joel, being the bearer of the horrific news. Joel and Dad commuted together back to Bayside to break the news to Mom.

Of course we were scared that this might precipitate another heart attack. She did not have a heart attack, but another kind of heartbreak began for our parents as they struggled to take in the enormity of Richie's diagnosis.

During this time all my helplessness crashed down on me. Joel in New York with our parents, me in Los Angeles sitting by Richie's bed watching his labored breathing through an oxygen mask, his once robust body withered by the loss of twenty pounds. I was paralyzed by the fear and pain in his blue eyes. How could I feel useful when all I was able to do was hold his hand and kiss his head?

Helplessness sucks. It left me reeling with the sense of my own massive impotence in the face of disease and death. It made me want to find Mr. Death and kick the crap out of him. Only I couldn't find him and like Orpheus wandering in ancient hallways seeking his dead Eurydice, I was only mortal and unable to change the will of the gods. Helplessness was knowing that AIDS spelled death and I couldn't change that.

Helplessness was listening to my mom telling me, months later, how she listened to Richie speaking about his depression and how she felt when he asked her the most excruciating question about ending his life.

"Sue, Richie asked me if I would be mad at him if he killed himself. What could I say? I told him I wouldn't be angry but I hoped he wouldn't kill himself. I said that maybe a cure or new drugs would be found, that maybe he would live a long, long time with AIDS." Then she began to cry.

Helplessness was mom weeping, 3,000 miles away and I could not reach out to hold her. Helplessness was mom saying, "Suzanne, parents are *supposed* to protect their children and I can't do that now. I can't even fly to see him while he is sick, my doctor forbids it, my heart is too weak to sustain air travel."

Helplessness was the anguished scream in the lithograph by Edward Munch.

TOXOPLASMOSIS

I cannot really know what it was like for Richie being diagnosed two days after his thirty-fourth birthday. After the KS diagnosis the denial I was carrying all those years began crumbling. With so many friends stricken and dying I had continued to push away the mere whisper of the thought that Richie would ever be one of those whose fate would be sealed with those dreaded words.

In May, a month after he was discharged from the hospital after his bout with PCP, Richie's illness took yet another horrific turn. For days he was distant and unreachable on the telephone. He was not returning phone calls regularly and when he did return them he sounded strange and detached. I assumed he was depressed but persisted in calling every day.

Mom called and asked me what was going on and I told her I didn't have a clue. We were worried but felt helpless to move him out of this odd state he was sinking into. It was late on a Thursday afternoon. I came home from my waitress job at Max's Diner, to a series of messages on my answering machine from Richie's friends. Both Joey and Mark sounded scared. I dialed Mark's number with a sense of foreboding.

"Hi Mark, it's Suzie'

"Hi Suzie, thank God you called, can you come down tonight? Richie is acting really strangely and we don't know what to do, he hasn't been answering phone calls and when I finally got him on the phone he sounded drugged. I went over there and—"

Mark's voice broke. Panic flooded me as I almost screamed,

"Mark, what's wrong?"

" I don't know, he was lying in the dark on the couch giggling to himself."

"In the dark?"

"Yes, the entire house was dark. I tried to talk to him but he just didn't seem to understand me."

"I'll be there as soon as I get a flight. I'll call you back."

With obvious relief in his voice Mark hung up. I called his doctor's office and spoke with his nurse. She put me on hold and then the doctor came on the line. I told him what Mark had said. "Suzanne, call me in the morning and we will try to get a bed for Richard at Sherman Oaks, take care of yourself and Richie."

I called PSA to book my flight to Burbank and then called Joel and Wendy.

"Hi Joel, it's me, Richie's sick again. Mark and Joey called me. He's acting weird."

Silence. Then Joel's voice came over the line. "When are you flying down?"

"Tonight. I'll call you and Wendy in the morning. Don't tell Mom or Dad yet."

Both Wendy and Joel's voices intermingled as they each said, "Kiss him for me, and take good care of yourself too." "I will, gotta go." My tears choked my voice when I called my housemate and friend, Barb, to tell her I wouldn't be home when she arrived from work. Echoing my brother and Wendy she said softly, "Sue, take good care of yourself and hug Richie for me." "I will Barb, I will."

Hours later I arrived in Burbank where Mark was waiting for me in his car.

"Who's with Richie?"

"Joey is there but he's scared to be alone with him."

"Scared?"

"Well, Richie is acting really weirdly, you'll see."

We drove in silence to Silverlake.

Joey was obviously relieved when he saw me at the door. To my brother's friends I was the cavalry coming to the rescue and a break from their overwhelming ordeal. I too was scared but maybe my presence would in some way help Richie.

He was on the couch sitting in front of the television. He looked up at me, smiled and said, "Suzie, hi."

Richie wasn't surprised to see me, which was also odd. Bending down to kiss him I noticed he was unshaven and unbathed. This alone was a sign that things were not right.

He was meticulous about his appearance and the odor that hit my nose was a huge shock. I kissed his cheek and sat down next to him. He had on an old leather jacket draped upside down on his chest and he was giggling.

I looked into his eyes and they were far, far away and vacant. Terror rippled through my body and my heart pounded. What was happening to my brother? I got up and walked Mark and Joey to the door.

Trying to reassure them—when it was me who really needed the most reassurance I told them,

"I'll call the hospital tomorrow and see if there is a bed for him "

Mark hugged me and gave me an offer that neither of us knew I would desperately need the next day.

"Call me tomorrow. I'll be home all day if you need any help I'll come over." I nodded my thanks with tears in my eyes and we hugged again. I sank down on the couch next to Richie and he reached for my hand. A play was on PBS and he began asking me questions about it. Only the questions made no sense and as I tried to answer him I knew that my brother was lost somewhere and that he had begun slipping away during the weeks that had preceded this night. Would he ever return or was this the end of both his mind and his life? My thoughts were interrupted by his murmuring and he turned to look at me with eyes that suddenly seemed very young and very confused. A smile wreathed his face as if he was very happy and pleased with himself.

"Suzie, isn't that wonderful? That is..."

His next words were unintelligible and his face shone with an unearthly glow. I didn't understand where my brother was and what was wreaking havoc with his once fine and brilliant mind. I only knew he was reaching out to me from whatever strange land he was lost in. Reaching out as he had all the years of our lives together, reaching out by sharing some strange and wonderful perspective on life as he saw it.

"Yes Richie, it is wonderful, yes my dear, dear brother, it truly is."

I pulled him to me in a fierce embrace and we sat there watching television and speaking inanities until he fell asleep.

The nightmare began again the next day when he refused to leave his bedroom and lay in bed in the dark talking to himself. I made frantic phone calls to his doctor's office but all they kept saying was there was no bed for him at the hospital until the next day. I was sitting staring unseeingly at Silverlake reservoir when the doorbell rang. I opened the door to someone I didn't recognize.

"Hi Suzanne, I'm Ben Ten, Richie's boss from Disney." I didn't know what to say, of all times to show up to see Richie.

"Hi, Ben, come on in, Richie's acting very strangely. I'm waiting to take him to the hospital tomorrow once a bed is available. It's not the greatest time to see him-"

"I'd still like to say hi, we miss him at the studio." Ben went into Richie's room and emerged in seconds, visibly shaken. As he sat on the sofa in the living room he looked at me with questioning eyes,

"God, what's wrong with him? "

"I don't know. It's so scary and we can't bring him to the hospital until tomorrow. I'll call you once I know what's going on." Ben gazed at me thoughtfully for what seemed an eternity. Then he asked the question I was dreading.

"Richard has AIDS doesn't he?"

I looked at this man who cared about my brother. I knew Richie had not told many people at Disney about his diagnosis, partly to protect his job and partly because he didn't want to come out as a gay male to his entire workplace; although some of them knew, many did not, or at least that's what Richie believed; he felt it was none of their business. Richie's not disclosing his illness was also a way to hold on to the hope that he would return to work and his position as Director of Home Video. Yet here in his home was his boss and friend and I was torn about how to respond. I said nothing but tears began trickling down my face. Ben's eyes filled with tears as he handed me an envelope.

"Here's a card for Richard. If you need *anything* please call. I'll be in the office tomorrow let me know what the doctor says."

Ben left and I was alone again. I tiptoed to Richie's bedroom. He was sleeping and when he woke up it was apparent he was slipping further away into some madness in his mind.

The next morning the hospital called. A bed was ready and they wanted us there by one in the afternoon. I went into Richie's dark room where he lay staring into space talking to himself.

"Richie? We're going to the hospital in a few hours so let's get you up and showered and shaved and I'll make you breakfast."

He stared vacantly at me and then he said, "I'm not going anywhere."

I stood there gaping, looking down at him and then I snapped; my brother was gone and I couldn't bear it any longer. All my fear, worry, sorrow and anger flooded through me and I began yelling.

"You ARE getting up damn it, and YOU ARE going to the hospital and you WILL shower and—"

He silently turned away from me. I realized then as my denial shattered around me like so many shards of glass that he was sicker than I could imagine. He began mumbling to himself as I ran out of his room in terror and called Joel.

Poor Joel. What could he do for me three thousand miles away in Connecticut? I desperately needed to know I was not alone and the sound of his voice soothed me for a moment.

"Let me try to talk to him—maybe he'll listen to me." Not surprisingly Richie wouldn't even look at me when I told him Joel was on the phone. I hung up and called Richie's therapist, Jim. Jim vetoed the idea of getting Richie into a psychiatric hospital.

"Suzanne he's very ill, he needs to be at Sherman Oaks, it's awful they waited this long to admit him. Call an ambulance service maybe they can get him there."

Within thirty minutes two emergency techs arrived and I

explained the situation to them- omitting the fact that Richie had AIDS. God only knew what they would have done then, probably run for their lives in terror.

These were the early dark and horrible years of AIDS in the 1980's; when people were thrown off airplanes and not allowed to fly if they were known to have AIDS; when hemophiliac children who contracted AIDS, because of tainted blood transfusions, were thrown out of schools, when their homes were burned to the ground; AIDS, ignored for years in Africa, shrugged away as the "wasting disease" because who cares anyway about anyone in Africa? This was how we lived back then, with AIDS, come to burrow into our bodies, our cells, our lives.

The techs couldn't get Richie to budge out of his bed.

"Come on Richard, look at your sister there, you don't want her to be upset anymore do you?" He stared at them and at me and then very quietly said, "Fuck off."

I walked them to the front door.

"Look miss, we can't take him forcibly, you're going to have to find another way to do this, we're sorry we couldn't be of any help to you both."

I was alone again staring out the cathedral windows at Silver Lake Reservoir shimmering serenely in the late morning sun. I slid open the glass door and sat on his terrace weeping. Finally I remembered Mark. Call Mark, maybe he could help. I had no one left to turn to. Joey was at work across town somewhere but Mark was home.

He arrived in fifteen minutes and walked into Richie's bedroom while I sat staring sightlessly at the view. Then I heard the shower water running. I walked back in to Richie's room where Mark was opening the blinds and windows. Turning to look at me he said, "Boy it stinks in here Suzie. He really needed a shower."

"Mark, what did you say to him, how did you-?"

"I don't know, maybe he was ready, but I told him if he didn't get up I was going to pull him out of bed, strip off his clothes and take him into the shower with me. Maybe that scared him." Mark grinned and I ran into his arms and we hugged for what seemed like an eternity.

Within an hour we were in Mark's car. Richie sat in front and after I hooked his seat belt I sat in the back seat. Richie reached his hand across his shoulder and we held hands the entire drive to the valley.

In the hospital the staff greeted us warmly and with that odd pity of staff who know that there is really nothing to smile about; but their smiles dissolved into shock and dismay when they saw the visible changes in Richie's appearance and demeanor. Once inside his room he refused to undress. I was coaxing him along until he refused to give me his jewelry. Leaning towards me he whispered, "They steal things here."

"Yes they do Richie, that's why you need to let me take your jewelry home with me where it'll be safe." He looked at me for a long time then slowly undid his wristwatch and his gold chain with the crystal that he wore around his neck. I left to tell the nurse he was in bed and ready for them. When I returned he was laying upside-down in the bed with his feet on the wall. I began to cry and the nurse held me as she steered me out the door.

"Suzanne we're going to take him outside for an MRI. Will you be able to come along?"

"What's an MRI?"

"It's a very new and sophisticated machine that takes

pictures of the brain, or any part of the body. The machine is outside the hospital in the lot behind us. Someone will be here to wheel your brother out but you can go along with him."

Of course I went to the MRI with Richie. I wasn't about to leave him alone after all this. I stood alongside the technicians as they took pictures of his brain. Even through his altered state he was scared and the tech spoke soothingly to him throughout the procedure. Hours later his doctor came to see me and Mark. His worried face spoke before he did.

"Suzanne, Mark, Richie has toxoplasmosis, a parasitic infection that we sometimes see in people with A.I.D.S. The parasite is attacking his brain and we can offer only one kind of treatment, which like all treatments is quite toxic." I looked at the doctor and said, "When will you start treatment?"

"Immediately, and hopefully we can stop whatever damage has begun from going further."

Treatment began and Joel flew to L.A. the next day. He hated hospitals but he moved past his fear and was there every day by Richie's bedside where Richie laid upside- down, feet on the wall, chatting in word—salad language we couldn't understand. Then he began talking in obscenities and calling everyone names. Joel and I looked at one another and burst out laughing and then I began sobbing, this was not Richie talking; his brain was totally screwed up from the damn parasite. The nurse ran into the room.

"What's going on? Richard?"

"Hey you pussy, who are you?" Stunned silence greeted his outburst. Then she turned to us smiling.

"That's okay. Don't worry. This behavior will stop as soon as the medication begins taking effect, but his brain is still under siege, be patient."

Richie began mumbling to himself. I walked over to the

window and gazed at the parking lot below. The nurse walked over and put her hands on my shoulders. My thoughts were overwhelming. *When would the nightmare stop? What next for Richie, for me, for our family?*

Over the days that followed I tormented myself. Why didn't the doctor put him in the hospital sooner? Why didn't I fly down the week before when he was sounding so distant and depressed?

In looking back I know that these thoughts were as futile then as they are now, a few years later. They are just another way to hold onto him and not let him go. The past and its "shoulda's, coulda's, woulda's" only punish myself in the present. Richie is gone and nothing can be done to change any of the things I did or didn't do right or wrong. I know that no amount of early intervention could have stopped Richie's immune system from crumbling. He had been living his life full-speed for years; even with night sweats, fevers, chills, and swollen glands; once the diagnosis was given his inner and outer defenses began crumbling. So when my mind tries to pull me into that path I say "NO."

"Leave me alone, I have suffered enough."

But there was no end in sight for Richie's suffering. He was discharged from the hospital weeks later with slight memory loss and a limp to his gait. It was awful. The parasite had done its damage, and my rage at his doctor's seemingly slow response to what he needed weeks before, barely subsided. I was angry at the world. My brother, my baby brother was fighting a disease we knew so little about. Couldn't someone please help him? God where are you? What is going on? Why is this happening to him, to us, to the world?

MEMORIAL DAY WEEKEND

I was visiting Richie for the holiday weekend. On Friday morning he woke up with excruciating pain in his mouth, the herpes outbreak he had been treated for earlier that week had spread to his esophagus. I watched as he bravely tried to eat breakfast, which consisted of rolling *Wonder Bread* into tiny balls so he could swallow them with water. "Richie, is there anything I can do for you? Maybe eating something softer, like a soft scrambled egg?" He looked at me with tears in his eyes. "Sue, I can barely swallow water. Just let me try eating this."

He hated *Wonder Bread* but it was impossible for him to digest his beloved *Wheat Berry* bread. He'd begun eating *Wonder Bread* after his last hospital visit. He needed to have something in his stomach in order to take his medicine and his vitamins. He was terrified of losing weight and was extremely proud of the weight he'd gained back since April. I sat watching him rolling endless balls of bread until I couldn't take it anymore. I went onto the deck—a scream stuck in my throat, stifling all the screams I felt inside my head and heart.

I walked back in. "Richie, I'm calling your doctor's office, there must be a better pain killer they can give you until this outbreak heals." He shrugged his shoulders at me, "Sure go ahead, try, I don't know how long I can stand this pain in my throat."

I spent hours on the phone trying to connect with Dr. Parker's partner since Dr. Joel, as Richie called him, was out of town. Finally the service reached him and he called. Richie needed intravenous methadone since the morphine wasn't blocking his pain. But now we needed to find a nurse's registry to administer the drug.

The Friday of Memorial Day weekend was not a good time to find home medical care. I spent more time on the phone trying to find a service that had someone available at such short notice. The remainder of the day and the night passed in complete and utter agony for Richie. The nurse arrived early Saturday morning. Dad arrived that afternoon from New York. Joey picked him up from the airport. He walked in looking exhausted and scared. The only other time I saw dad looking scared was the night of Mom's heart attack. It was hard for me to know what to say or do. So I did the only thing I could do. I went up to my father and hugged him.

"Dad, I'm so glad you're here. You must be tired." Then he asked, "How's Richie feeling, did they give him a painkiller to help?"

"They sent a nurse from the registry. She's in his room setting up the I.V. drip. Go in and see him before he falls asleep from the drug." I knew he was scared to see Richie and it wasn't just because of AIDS. What do you say to your son who is so ill? What words do you use to connect when you know your child may soon die? I don't know what he said in the privacy of Richie's room but the visit meant so much to Richie. He was resigned to Mom's being restricted from flying since her heart attack but his longing to see her and his friends in New York increased tenfold after Dad flew back east later that week.

I flew home to San Francisco on Memorial Day. The next day I went to work. I walked from the Montgomery Street BART station to Max's, which was on Folsom and 3rd street. By the time I reached the restaurant I was in tears, shaking and barely able to talk. My manager Susan steered me into her office.

"Suzanne, let me make you some tea and toast, okay?" I nodded to her. Her voice became even gentler, "Suzanne, is there someone who can take you home from here, someone you can call?"

I whispered, "Yes, Marlene, I think she's home from work today." Susan nodded at me, "Great, there's the phone, call her while I get you something to munch on." I picked up the phone and punched in the number, Marlene answered instantly.

"Hi Mar, it's me, Suzanne-" I began to cry. Marlene's worried voice came over the line. "Suz, what's wrong, how's Richie? What's-"

"Mar? Can you pick me up at Max's Diner and take me home? I'm too exhausted to be here."

She arrived in a half-hour and drove me to my apartment in Noe Valley. I stumbled into bed and slept twelve hours. Richie was alone after Dad flew back East. His nurse Scott was there with him during the day but the evening nurses were nightmares. One nurse stole jewelry, one nurse stole Richie's pain medication and finally we begged the service to allow Scot to work full-time.

SCOTT

I loved Scott B. He was not an R.N. but a poorly paid L.V.N. who came to us through the home care service that Richie needed more and more frequently since his bout with toxoplasmosis. Scott's presence alleviated some of Richie's terror and loneliness. He and Scott didn't get along all the time but each of them seemed to get a kick out of the differences that caused arguments. Scott was from a small town in Florida and his views on life were vastly different from Richie's; but Scott was there for Richie on those interminable weekdays when no one visited and on Saturday nights when his friends were out dancing and doing all the things Richie used to do before his life began shattering into pieces all around him.

I often felt a stab of piercing loneliness when I hung up the phone after talking with Richie. The miles to Los Angeles felt as far away as the moon. We talked about my moving to L.A. or his moving to San Francisco but it didn't happen. Events moved so swiftly and truth be told I did not want to uproot my life and move in with Richie. I felt like a very selfish sister, how could I *not* move down there, how could I *not* be willing to live with him? Some part of me was afraid we would tear each other up if we lived together, we were still arguing and fighting at times and the thought of having that escalate scared me; I also did not want to leave my graduate school studies indefinitely, at this point they were on hold for two quarters so I could be more available to Richie.

I felt really crappy when I told him I wasn't going to move down, in fact I don't even recall our conversation; he must have felt devastated but he never reproached me about my decision; on his last visit to the Bay area we looked at apartments for him but of course he didn't want to leave his life in L.A., his work, his friends and, most of all, his doctor.

My therapist Lorraine again said to me, "Suzanne, this isn't some made-for-T.V.-movie where everything works out and life is ideal. Stop beating yourself up for fighting with Richie, for the choices you are making, you are doing the best you can with circumstances wildly beyond your control." Some friends say I wasn't selfish. They say I was there for my brother and he knew that. I know, once again, that the road to re-examining my choices, of re-hashing the past is a cruel pastime laced with guilt.

HOME

In June we decided that a trip home to see Mom and Dad Joel, Wendy and his beloved nieces, four year old Nicole, and one year old Tracey, should happen fast. With so much uncertainty about Richie's health we were holding off booking the flight, thinking that a last-minute flight was probably best.

The week we were deciding when to fly to New York Richie's social worker, Pam, from Sherman Oaks Hospital, called while I was working at Max's. She left me a message asking me to call her as soon as possible.

I stood in a phone booth on Market Street calling her office and wondering why she'd called. Richie spoke with her intermittently when he needed help with the various papers and forms that needed filling out for his home care. Maybe he'd called her this week.

"Hi Pam, Did Richie told you we're flying to New York to see our family? We're still trying to figure out when to book our flight, so that's my news, what did you want to talk to me about?"

"Suzanne, you ought to go as soon as you can, you know the prognosis for him. Now that he's had toxo once it's two to six months for the parasite to return and most don't survive a second go round with it."

Stunned I looked out the phone booth at the traffic on Market Street. I felt as if the world had suddenly slowed down to a strange and distant crawling of time, the same feeling I'd had in a car accident when I was nineteen; whirling in the vortex of the car's spinning, all of life seemingly slowing down to the crash that was building up. When the two cars hit the sounds exploded in my head like a freight train's roar- the crescendo deafening me as my consciousness returned to real time. This felt similar when suddenly I heard the car horns on the street, the sounds of the buses roaring past the phone booth.

"What did you say? What are you talking about? His doctor didn't say one word to us about this. Are you crazy? Two to six months?"

"Suzanne, I am so sorry, I thought you knew."

"KNEW? You thought I knew? What are you saying?"

" I'm saying that the sooner you can make the trip the better. There is no treatment to stop the disease from recurring after the initial bout. I am so sorry Suzanne. I am so sorry Richie's doctor didn't say anything to you or Joel or Richie."

I hung up the phone and pressed my head against the door. She must have the facts all screwed up, this was just not possible. The feeling of déjà vu enveloped me as I walked to the BART station. I don't remember my ride to Mission Street or my transferring to the bus taking me to Noe Valley.

That night I told Sarah the news. I couldn't bring myself to speak to my family, and Richie; what was I going to do about Richie? I woke the next day determined to call Joel and talk with him before Richie or our parents. Joel solved my dilemma by calling me while I was still drinking my morning tea.

"Hi Sue, thought I'd let you know Wendy and I are thinking of moving to L.A. in the late fall to be near Richie." I thought to myself it's now or never.

"Joel I have something to tell you, it is really awful, but I spoke with Pam yesterday, you know, Richie's' social worker at the hospital?"

Before he could respond I rushed on, my words tumbling and stumbling. I felt sick to my stomach. "She says that the prognosis for someone who has had one bout of toxo is two to six months."

The phone was silent at Joel's end.

"Joel I'm so sorry to have to tell you this I just don't know what to do, how to tell Richie, I am so furious at—" Joel's voice exploded.

"The hell with her. What does she know? SHE ISN"T A DOCTOR."

I waited a moment and then said, "Joel, why didn't the doctor tell us and Richie about this? What are we going to do?"

His voice, much subdued, asked me the question I wanted him to help me resolve.

"Richie doesn't know? What are you going to do, when will you tell him? Are you going to tell him?"

"No, I told Sarah last night. I was going to call you after breakfast. What can I do? I don't want to tell him. He wants to fly to New York to see you and everyone and I think we should just book the flight and go; and the sooner the better. Why tell him? He's so depressed. What would he do any differently if he knew? His doctor is such a coward not telling him or us, or maybe he also thinks there's no point in telling Richie. But damn it, he still should have talked with us. I don't know if I should even bother talking to the doctor I'm furious at him, letting Pam do his "dirty work" because that's how this feels to me." We ended our call with very little left to say to each other.

I called Richie later in the day, feeling very weird about the knowledge I now held inside but I really thought it was for the best. He was suffering so much mental anguish I just couldn't bring myself to talk with him, especially over the phone, about something as horrendous as this latest turn of events.

We decided to book the flight to New York for the following week. I told Susan and Bob, the head manager at Max's, that I needed to take time off to fly home with Richie. They were so wonderful. Most restaurants would have fired someone in my circumstances by now but they told me not to worry and that my job was still mine when I returned.

Dad and Mom purchased first class one way tickets for our flight, they wanted Richie to be comfortable and thank God they were able to afford this gift. We had no idea how Richie's health would hold up while we were visiting so leaving our return date open-ended seemed best.

I arrived in L.A. the day before our flight to New York but the next day our early morning flight plans turned into a nightmare. The flight was delayed four hours and Richie wasn't feeling well. I begged the airline personnel to let us into the members only TWA Sky Lounge, and when they saw how shaky and pale Richie was they relented and allowed us inside. By the time we boarded the flight it was four hours later.

He was exhausted. Our lousy luck that the first class cabin had a party of six women and men who began drinking the moment they boarded, and continued drinking until the plane landed at JFK airport. They were loud, obnoxious and drunk the entire flight. I wanted to kill them. The flight personnel were unable to contain them. When Richie left his seat to use the restroom an attendant came over to me. Pointing at the pill bottles on his tray she asked if he was very ill.

In 1986 people were refused seats on airplanes or asked to disembark, when it was discovered that they had AIDS. I nodded at her and smiled sadly, which was not difficult to do.

"Well my brother had a bad case of bronchitis but it's over now."

"Okay, but if you need anything just holler. Or don't—it's already noisy here."

I smiled up at her.

"Looks like your hands are full with that crowd."

She made a face in their direction and we both laughed.

"Yup, the entire crew is ready to jettison them out the door. Okay, again, don't hesitate to ask for anything, we have plenty of booze as you know, and food and sweets. Hope your brother feels better."

It felt good to share a laugh and I felt less alone for the moment. When Richie returned I told him about the conversation.

He dozed fitfully the entire way to New York only waking now and then to make sure I was enjoying my experience in first class. He flew first class for his many business trips and was amused by my wonder at the endless offerings of liquor, candies, cakes and other food.

We landed at JFK at ten p.m. instead of four in the afternoon as originally scheduled. Mom and Dad were waiting in a limousine Dad's company hired and insisted they use to pick us up. It was his boss' way of giving my parents support. All he knew was that Richie was sick with cancer. Coming out of the closet about Richie's diagnosis and his sexual orientation was, understandably, not something my dad wanted to deal with at his office. The dismay on their faces when they saw Richie was apparent as they swept both of us up into their arms for hugs.

During our visit Mom and Dad took me aside to ask about Richie. Their looks of grief and pain were excruciating for me to witness.. I answered their questions as best I could.

"It's so very day to day, we don't know from one moment to the next what is going to happen."

I couldn't talk with them about what the social worker told me about the toxoplasmosis recurring. After all, what did she know? She wasn't a doctor and even doctors guess at diagnoses and outcomes.

Richie wasn't able to leave the house the entire time we visited. His friend Tommy commuted from Manhattan on the Long Island Railroad for a few visits.

On his last visit I drove him to the train station a few miles from my parent's home. "Suzie, how is he really doing?" Tommy's beautiful brown eyes filled with tears as I told him about the prognosis and then we both broke down and cried in each other's arms. We knew it was probably the last time he would see Richie.

During our visit I witnessed the wordless pain in our parent's eyes. My mother's already physically broken heart must have been emotionally breaking over and over again with the pain of seeing her once vital, talkative, witty son huddled in pain under his blanket on the living room couch; and how her heart must have shattered again as she bent down to kiss him goodbye one more time at the airport when we flew back to California.

My dad's heart, already heavy from concern and worry about mom's health and reeling from his recent visit to Richie in May must have also shattered with his helplessness to save his son from the disease that was destroying him inch by inch.

Once active in "Parents of Gays" they had stopped going to their meetings. I worried that they had little support for themselves. The neighbors, like Dad's officemates, also thought Richie had cancer, even my mom's closest friends did not know the truth. Unfortunately Pam the social worker had been right with her bleak news. Our parents never saw Richie again.

AUGUST IS THE CRUELEST MONTH

The phone jolted us awake and Sarah leaped out of bed to answer it. It was seven a.m. Saturday, August 9, a date I will never forget. Through my half—awake state I heard her say, "Who is it? Hi Scott, hang on." With worried eyes she handed me the phone as I stumbled into the kitchen.

"Hi Scott. What's wrong?'"

"Suzanne, I'm bringing Richie to the hospital. Please call the doctor's service. He's acting very strangely. I think it's toxo again." I froze when I heard Scott's words. I was screaming inside when I replied in a whisper, "O God, no, not toxo. Yes, I'll call the service. We'll get a flight out. I'll see if Joey can pick us up at Burbank. See you in a few hours. Thank you Scott, I don't know what we'd do without you."

After a flurry of phone calls we packed our clothing and our dirty laundry and drove to Oakland airport. Saturday was laundry day and Sarah decided that while I was at the hospital she'd stay at Richie's place and do our laundry. I knew she was overwhelmed from the past six months of crisis after crisis and doing laundry was her way of coping; to try to do something normal and familiar. Her willingness to fly down to L.A. meant so much to me but for me there was nothing normal or familiar that could offer any solace. Sarah's presence was my solace.

Joey was waiting for us at the airport. We stopped at the hospital to drop me off.

Walking into the room we found Scott dozing in a chair by Richie's bedside. I thought Richie was also asleep but he opened his eyes, smiled at me and said "Hi Suzie." Those were the last words I ever heard him speak. Richie lapsed into coma from that moment on.

Although toxoplasmosis was again suspected as the cause of his coma, the nurses around me were muttering that they didn't understand why the doctor wasn't medicating Richie or ordering any tests to confirm the diagnosis. I was upset and angry about it but there didn't seem to be any recourse except to wait. Sarah flew back to Oakland late Sunday afternoon. Joel was arriving on Tuesday and for now I was alone and very scared

On Monday an MRI was ordered. Richie was still in coma and vomiting the entire way down to the test. I wiped his mouth over and over again as we wheeled him to the MRI building. I was worrying about the germs in the air outside the hospital as the smoggy air hit my lungs. I was in shock. Imagine worrying about more germs harming him when he was already so ill. I wanted so much to control the world around him and keep him safe but I really couldn't do that. All I could do was worry and wipe vomit from his lips. Helplessness swept over me in waves and by the time we reached the door to the facility I was weeping. The nurse and technician were so kind, offering me sodas and cookies. Although I turned the offerings down it was a relief to have someone take care of me, even if only for a moment.

The MRI proved what we already knew. The parasite was again relentlessly attacking Richie's brain. Later that day the doctor called me on the phone in Richie's room. He wanted to talk with Joel and me on Tuesday. A sense of dread and foreboding filled me. I called Mom and Dad and told them the results of the test and that no treatment was being given Richie and the doctor wanted to talk to me and Joel. Silence hummed along the phone line. I broke it.

"Look, I don't know what's going on but maybe," my voice cracked.' Maybe we have to expect the very worst."

I couldn't name it, I couldn't say it aloud. I couldn't get my brain to form the words which would travel to my tongue and explode into sound and meaning. Richie was dying. I couldn't say it. I began crying.

I'd sat in that same phone booth on and off over the last six months clutching the receiver in my hand and staring into the hospital lobby watching people coming and going as they entered and left the elevators. I'd sat in that phone booth calling my parents, Joel, Sarah, friends and work. I 'd given bad news and sort of good news to everyone and shared my terror over countless long distance phone calls but nothing, nothing compared to this moment.

I sat there sobbing to my mom and dad because we all knew he was dying. How could I say the words aloud, tell them their baby son was dying? How could I do it? My tears did it for me and in the end it didn't matter because they knew it anyway.

I returned to his bedside and sat there alone in the darkening room until late at night when I left to drive back to Silverlake. I thought about sleeping by his side but I just couldn't do it. I wasn't thinking clearly at all and I couldn't figure out what to do, to stay by his side all night or to leave, finally I drove home at midnight.

Tuesday morning Kevin, Richie's buddy from the AIDS Project L.A., came to drive me to LAX to pick up Joel. Kevin treated me to lunch in a 1950's style café similar to Max's Diner, hoping it would help me feel better. I drank a vanilla malted and ate French fries with my grilled cheese sandwich. But even my comfort food offered little solace.

Kevin's hand holding mine as we drove to the airport was the comfort I sought and needed. Kevin was another angel-boy, the same as Scott. He and Richie hit it off and when Richie could leave the house they went shopping and to the movies. I was grateful beyond words for Kevin's presence in Richie's life. Kevin also had AIDS but was able to get around and do things that Richie couldn't do.

The August heat and smog were unbearable the closer we got to the airport. I ran to Joel and we hugged tightly; I climbed into the tiny backseat of Kevin's car. I liked the back seat because it gave me a chance to space out and not have to talk much. Joel began crying and I reached my hand out and held his shoulder the entire ride to the hospital. When we arrived I left Joel in the room alone with Richie and his sobs shattered the quiet of the floor. A nurse came running and I barred his entrance to the room.

"Michael please don't go in. It's our brother, Joel. It's okay; please don't go in, he needs to be alone with Richie." We heard Joel imploring Richie to talk to him and then more sobbing as only silence greeted his entreaties. I began crying and Michael held me in his arms.

Joel finally emerged and we went to wait for Dr. Parker in the only empty patient room on the floor. At this time there wasn't even a lounge for family and friends to wait in as the ward was running out of rooms for beds. I often visited the nurse's station or sat on an empty gurney when I took a break from Richie's side.

The doctor finally joined us. The afternoon sunlight was streaming through the window as Joel and I leaned against the wall. The conversation took less than twenty minutes. He looked uncomfortable as he began talking to us.

"Richard has toxoplasmosis again. I honestly don't know what he will be like after this bout. It's attacking a different part of his brain then it did in May, and his speech as well as more of his walking may be permanently damaged. What I'm asking you to decide is if we should medicate him or not."

I stared at the doctor. I was fuming inside beneath my sorrow and numbness.

"Why have you withheld medication for two days? Isn't that making it worse?"

"Suzanne, the truth is that your brother is very sick and even if we can pull him out of this we'll be standing here again in a few months or weeks, facing yet another disease or this one again. His immune system is shot and all of you, especially Richard, will have to go through this again and again. I think it would be best to let him go now. He's not going to live long and with each illness his time gets shorter."

A stunned silence met the doctor's words. Joel told him we'd get back to him the next morning. Joel was legal and medical power of attorney for Richie. After his near-death in May from toxoplasmosis he'd finally agreed to create a will. Joel teased me about my not being named power of attorney. I think he just didn't know what to say and neither did I.

"See, he made me in charge because he was afraid you'd say, 'sure, go ahead and let him die, there is an afterlife.'"

"Not funny Joel, not funny." I began to cry.

The doctor had given us a mind-numbing decision to make. We called Mom and Dad and they had little to say, for what was there to say now? Nothing more could be done or said that would change anything.

Later that day Richie's therapist, Jim, showed up at the hospital. He told me that Richie was one of his most depressed AIDS clients.

"You know Suzanne, once he stopped working at Disney, well that began killing him as much as knowing he had AIDS." I nodded mutely. Jim visited Richie every time he was hospitalized and I had taken him up on his offer to call if I needed support when I was in L.A. Poor Jim, his lover had died of AIDS the week before and his entire practice was being torn apart by the onslaught of AIDS among his clients. Yet here he was offering one more person support and love.

That evening after leaving the hospital we stopped in a bar in Silverlake. After settling onto the barstools Joel beckoned the bartender over.

"Would you be able to help us make a big decision?"

The bartender stared at Joel as if he'd grown antennas.

"Are you nuts?"

"Well, I thought that was part of a bartender's job."

"Look buddy, this ain't a movie and that's not my job." Shaking his head he walked to the other end of the bar.

Joel turned to me and said, "Well kid what do we do? Medicate him or not?"

"I think the doctor's right. In a few months or weeks we'll be here again, and again. Richie wants his life back the way it was. That's never going to happen. Not being able to work is also killing him. You heard the doctor, 'Richie wants to go back to the studio to work and that's not going to happen. His depression is overwhelming him. No medication is helping that."

"Shit, Sue, why do you have to have such a good memory? This sucks..."

I didn't respond. It was all surreal. Here we were in a bar talking about ending our brother's life. This was nuts. Life wasn't supposed to be like this, was it? We left the bar an hour later and Joel refused to come upstairs to Richie's condo with me. I was worried about him driving around without me.

"Joel, I can't take much more. Please drive carefully."

He nodded and smiled, driving off with a squeal of rubber.

I lay awake until he came home after one a.m. He stumbled into the living room.

"Are you awake?"

"Of course I am."

"This sucks doesn't it?"

"There are no words to describe it and I just wish it would all go away."

"You know what we have to do, are you sure this is right?"

"Joel I'm not sure of anything. He's already gone without medication for days now.

You know and I know that he's just going to get sick again and again until he dies. Maybe we need to let him go—."

Sobs tore my words to shreds. Joel reached over the back of the couch and patted my head.

"See you in the morning kid."

"Yeah, in the morning."

In the morning we talked with Dr. Parker and told him we agreed with Richie's Living Will. Richie would never walk into his office at Disney Studios, never dance again in a crowded bar with Joey and Mark, making silly jokes about men's shoes; he would never hold my hand as we walked along Melrose avenue window shopping until I became bored and cranky. Richie's quality of life was gone—never to return. It was time to let him go, the battle with AIDS was over.

WEDNESDAY AUGUST 14

I remember getting lost after leaving the hospital. I was crying so hard that I took a wrong turn and ended up on the wrong freeway. I had never driven a car with a fifth gear and Richie's Honda Prelude had five gears. I was terrified I was going to break the car if I didn't shift into fifth gear. Trouble was I couldn't find fifth gear. I was driving with tears streaming down my face, on a freeway I didn't know. I finally left the freeway and found my way home on the unfamiliar Los Angeles streets-driving in third and fourth gear all the way. When I walked in Joel was standing in the kitchen looking as haggard as I felt.

"Hi Sue, I'm exhausted from dealing with Richie's papers, do you want to get something to eat?"

"Sure, I forgot to eat lunch. Joel? Is it okay to drive the car in fourth gear and not use fifth gear? I got so scared, I couldn't shift into fifth and I thought I was destroying the engine not using that gear." Joel usually used any opportunity for a joke but this time he didn't. He was gentle as he said with a sad smile, "Don't worry; you can drive the car without fifth gear. It's there to help save gas having an engine go up to a higher gear. What difference does it make anyway? It's your car now, you know that."

I made a face at Joel and we went out for dinner. That night as I tossed and turned on the couch I thought about owning Richie's car. He loved his new Honda. What the hell was I doing with it? My world was upside-down. Nothing mattered. Not learning that I could drive and not use fifth gear, eating didn't matter, drinking didn't matter; I wanted my baby brother back, well and happy, and that was not going to happen so why care about anything, ever, ever again?

Sarah flew down on Friday after her work ended. The three of us had dinner and then she and I went to the hospital to sit with Richie.

Joel left for the East coast the next day. We held each other tightly. He was clutching a dish towel to wipe his tears. There was nothing left to say. He'd said goodbye to Richie. It was time for him to go home and be with Wendy and the children.

AUGUST 17

Richie's room felt like a chapel, there was a hushed silence reminiscent of holy places. The morning nurse asked me if I wanted to help her shave and bathe Richie. I will be forever grateful to that nameless angel for her loving offer. My shock was so enormous I didn't fully understand that we were preparing him for his death.

We shaved his beautiful face and I gently patted *Polo* cologne on his soft skin. I was so afraid I screwed up shaving his sideburns, not wanting to acknowledge that he would never wake up again, not even to scold me for messing up his hair. I kissed him as we lowered the bed and placed fresh pillows beneath his head.

Where to start? Where to end? It was now four fifteen in the afternoon. The room had grown unearthly still. Kevin and Sarah were seated alongside the bed. I was holding Richie, kissing him, stroking his face. I felt like a mother, only I wasn't giving birth, instead I was accompanying my brother on his last journey, it was his death I was "birthing" him to. I watched the pulse beating in his neck, until it stopped. Sliding off the bed and into a bedside chair I asked Sarah, and Kevin, to leave me alone; as the door closed I felt something, a presence, a pressure on my shoulder, a sense of urgency conveying itself to me, asking me, telling me to "turn, turn around, turn around."

The corner of the hospital room was blazing with golden light. Hours before I had closed the blinds to keep out the glare from the afternoon sun. I dimly understood the light was not of this world and it had everything to do with Richie. I turned back to gaze at Richie's body; turning again to look over my shoulder to the corner of the room. That light—it was still there. Then I looked back at Richie and when I turned around the light was gone. Vaguely, beyond my shock and grief, I knew that light was Richie telling me goodbye, telling me not to despair, because life and our spirits were bigger than the very sick, AIDS ravaged body, he had just left. Registering somewhere beyond my grief I remember thinking 'only dying people see the light when they leave their bodies, surely no one alive sees anything like this.'

It would take years for me to come to grips with the enormity of this gift, this glimpse into the realm beyond earthly form and substance. But at that time and place, a late summer afternoon in August of 1986 in a small hospital in Sherman Oaks, my awareness was narrowed down to the enormous waves of grief flooding my heart.

The rest of the day was a blur. Sarah couldn't stay in L.A. and I was so terrified of being alone I flew back with her to Oakland.

The nurses, Sarah, and Richie's friends didn't know how to treat me as they moved me into the car for the drive to the airport. I could see it all from afar as if I were surrounded by glass that was inches thick; surrounded by a great wall of silence and stillness through which I could see and hear everything.

I watched from this strange place I inhabited, nodding, speaking, smiling woodenly. I was safe behind that wall, it was so silent, so quiet. The stillness soothed and surrounded me, held me, rocked me like a baby. I longed for it to last forever and ever. But it didn't.

It broke with a great shuddering "whoosh," like the sudden roaring and then the dread silence as in the eye of a hurricane when all the world holds its breath, the spinning stops and the storm, seems motionless in its fury, great gusts of wind moving so fast that all is suspended high in the air like matchstick toys in some giant's ghastly unknowing hand.

The no longer silent fury of the storm now pummeling away and your insides feel as if they have been turned inside out and your head is slammed back from the wind, the awful wind, flattening you and everyone and everything in its path.

I heard the furious, keening moan from far, far away.

I heard the anguished wail penetrate and slice through the air. I heard it long before I knew it was myself I heard.

With a great deafening roar my glass wall broke and I felt the ripping open of my heart like some terrible, red, wound. I felt it spread and open until my body was one endless hole of anguish and pain.

I heard the long howling "No" streaming from my gaping mouth. I felt my vocal cords stretching almost beyond endurance with the word.

I looked down and saw my hands grasping the hot metal bars of the PSA gangway leading up to the plane. I felt hands on me, Sarah, trying in futility, to pry my fingers one by one off the bars.

"Nooo, I can't leave him, he's alone. No. Don't make me go."

Above me I sensed without seeing, the stewardess, and I saw below me, a line of passengers. The heat lay heavy on Los Angeles and all about us it shimmered and spun, the black tar sending it in great waves upward; the late afternoon sky looking like an inverted china bowl, blue and white, no wind, no clouds.

"Suzie, we've got to get on the plane."

"I can't leave him. I can't go."

"You must. He's gone now. We'll be back on Tuesday."

"O God, my baby brother, I can't leave him, please don't make me leave him."

Sarah's compassionate hazel eyes were filled with tears. "Suzie, please, come on the plane, there's nothing you can do now for Richie, let's go home. I can't stay tonight and I won't leave you here alone."

With great gulping cries I allowed her to lead me up the gangway and to our seats.

I sank into my seat, head against the window shade.

I remember three things about that flight.

When we were seated a flight attendant asked her what was wrong with me and she told her about Richie.

"I wish we had a quiet flight home for you but there's a high school soccer team on board who are celebrating their win."

Sarah smiled at the flight attendant. "That's okay, it's a quick flight, don't worry about us."

The soccer team was loud and raucous, but now and then above their noise my wailing could be heard. I huddled against the window, Sarah my buffer zone.

I remember the teen sitting on the aisle near Sarah, she was hearing impaired and pointed to me, gesturing to Sarah to ask what was wrong with me. Sarah wrote her a note explaining. The girl smiled sympathetically at me and spent her time creating two tiny green ribbons from the craft basket she had. I managed to smile and in American Sign Language lifted my hand to say "I love you." For years I kept my green ribbon attached to the shirt I wore the day Richie passed away.

I remember the woman who stuck her face into mine, straining past Sarah waving her hands to fend her off, as she asked me with a vampire-like interest, "What is going on with you? Her eyes sucking at me, the kind of woman who lingers on streets and freeways, breathing in the twisted art of cars and bodies grotesquely entwined after one terrible moment in time. The kind of person who seems to grow larger from the horror and grief of others. I don't know who told her but moments later we passed her in the airport as she stood in a phone booth, and I heard her saying, "You'll never believe what I just saw and heard, this woman on the plane was crying so loudly all the way from L.A..."

Even in my numbed state of mind I wished her dead instead of my brother. My thought was interrupted as our friend Helen, who had been waiting for our arrival, scooped Sarah and I up and the three of us clung together, seeking comfort where there was none to be found.

That night I sat on the floor of Sarah's kitchen sobbing into the phone to my parents. Aunt Florry and Uncle Vic called. They each told me to be strong and that Richie wanted me to take good care of myself. We three children were their children too since they had none of their own, the grief in their voices choked off the rest of our conversation.

The next day I began calling synagogues in L.A. to find a place for Richie's memorial service. I spoke with Janet Marder, she was the new rabbi at Temple Beth Chayim Chadsim in West L.A.; it was a synagogue that had a large congregation of gay men and women. She was a new rabbi and her ministry was consumed with funerals and memorials for all the men dying from AIDS. The memorial was set for Wednesday. I spoke to Joel, and Mom and Dad over and over again that day. But finally when my phone calls were over I was alone. I was totally and utterly alone on the West Coast. Richie no longer a short plane ride or phone call away. He was utterly beyond my reach.

I flew to L.A. with Sarah and Helen on Tuesday. On Wednesday Richie's body was cremated as we gathered in the synagogue to celebrate his life and mourn his passing. That morning over ninety people came together to honor his memory.

After the memorial we gathered at a Japanese restaurant to toast Richie and eat sushi in his memory. How he would have delighted in all the love pouring out towards him that day. So many lives he touched, so many hearts broken with grief.

SURVIVORSHIP

I have not been able to, nor have I wanted to, put pen to paper since August 17. As if by avoiding writing I can avoid confronting Richie's death. Even to write those words takes such an effort, all I feel is pain and sadness- the sorrow washing over me, through me and there is no end to it.

I awaken from sleep at 2 or 4 a.m. and think, "Oh no, there's been some terrible mistake- Richie is not gone." But it's no mistake and all I have is a vast desolation and a denial my mind repeats over and over—but my heart knows the truth. My brother is dead.

A thousand tiny impulses filter through each day, a thought, "I'll buy this for him", or, "I must remember to tell him..." and each impulse is left hanging on some jagged edge of grief, each thought left dangling, each moment ended abruptly. No. Never again will I laugh with him, hug him, hold his hand, hear his voice, hear our voices raised in argument, never again will we share anything. All is silence, and void, and sharp edges of memories. The real agony is that my life is going on, inexorably, day by day, and he is left behind, frozen in time, always 34, always the days before August 17; and I move on because I, however unwillingly, am alive.

I remember wanting to die, staring at the tracks of the BART train, the 3rd rail whispering my name, gripping the edge of the steel barrier, gazing longingly at the tracks. I remember driving across the Golden Gate Bridge with the image of stopping my car some fog-filled night, getting out and leaping into the dark below.

I remember driving my car, Richie's car, so recklessly, so fast, that autumn and winter that, by spring, the car needed a new clutch and transmission. I remember shouting until my throat was raw. Driving east on the freeway, then west, then east again, never going anywhere, just driving from exit to exit on and off the freeway for hours with the moon roof on the car open- screaming, sobbing my rage; the wind catching my grief and flinging it into the air as I drove like a woman possessed.

Dream—October 1986

Richie is wearing a white cowboy outfit with a sequined heart stitched on the pants which reads, "ILY." He looks happy, healthy and tanned. I awaken crying.

Dream- January 1987

Richie is eating vanilla ice cream. He is pale and we are at home. He is listening to a tape recording of his dying and saying to me, "It is all just an illusion, don't worry." I hear him gasping for breath between the words. I angrily hit him on the shoulder. Then I say, "See, no one wants to listen to this." I awaken crying.

FEBRUARY 26, 1987

Today is my 38th birthday. The first without Richie. No flowers will be sent, no phone call, no card, just the memory of other birthdays, and his love for me tucked away inside my heart.

Survivor's guilt is a funny thing. Memories swirl about me and most are about how I messed up and didn't do enough when he was ill. I beat myself up that I didn't stay for longer visits in L.A. when he had days of feeling well those last six months. I forget the bone-weary tiredness that was so much a part of me I thought I always felt this way. I forget that I needed to fly back to San Francisco to work at Max's Diner, to limp along in my graduate school classes. I forget that sometimes I needed a break from the fear I lived with of what next? I forget I just needed to sleep in my own bed and regroup. I forget because I am ashamed to admit I was not the perfectly attentive, I am here for you every minute, every day, sister. I forget because I really don't want to remember any of it. I don't want to remember him ill. I don't want to think about him being scared and overwhelmed.

APRIL 1988

In four months it will be two years. Two years has its own cruelty. Two years means that the last time I heard his voice, saw him, touched him was 1986. Two years means my life has gone on...without him. My eyes are so filled with tears I cannot see to type. Missing him never ceases. I long to hear him say, "Suzie, I am so proud of you finishing grad school. I am so proud of you writing again. Suzie, I love you, and hey, you look so pretty today."

I suffer from survivor's guilt because it distracts me from his absence in my life. If I stop beating myself up then I am left to sit, again and again, with what is. Yes, we fought. Yes, I was not there for him every day. Yes, we yelled at one another and got angry. Yes, we didn't always understand each other. Yes, I was furious with him for being sick. Yes, yes, yes. Yes. Richie is gone, and I? I am alive.

April 11, 1988

Dear Richie,

Have I told you how painful it is for me when the seasons change? Have I mentioned how it hurts to smell the new-green scent of spring in the air? Have I told you how pain slices through me when it is still light outside at 8 p.m. and a second summer without you is almost here?

Walking into my apartment a gypsy thought invades my brain, "I'll call Richie and see how-DAMNITOHELL". Even now, 20 months since you died, my mind plays tricks on me. I thought about buying you a Hanukkah present this December. I just can't seem to get it. Even now there is a piece of denial hanging about-even now all of me doesn't buy it, surely this isn't true? But it is true, sadly and finally true. You are not here and I walk on this Earth without you. I need you here to yell at me and say, "Suzie, stop analyzing everything." I need to hear you say, "Suzie, that novel you are writing, how is it going?" Mostly I just need you.

Richie, have I told you about Ocean Beach in San Francisco? That's where part of your ashes were scattered. Joel visited Seal Rock last year with his business associates and told me there seemed to be something magical about the place. I never told him that part of your ashes were scattered there on a cold night in December. My mind reels from these words. No. No. NO.

Not ashes, not ashes I also held in my hands on a wintry day along the shores of Long Island sound, also in December, only four months after you passed away. My friends Barbara and Cheryl drove me there that Sunday morning. I remember my feet getting wet as I stepped into the water lapping the sand. Your ashes in a tiny box, ashes, not who you really were.

Did I tell you that Fontelle had your ashes at her house for months before I went back to L.A? I left your ashes at the crematorium in August in my hurried and shell-shocked departure after your memorial service. The crematorium's airplane scattered some of your ashes over the ocean near L.A. I called your dear friend Fontelle and asked if she would be able to pick up the remaining ashes. She said she felt honored to keep them at her home until Sarah and I arrived back in L.A. She loved you so very much and still does.

Crematoriums are strange places. Did I tell you about my calling all these crematoriums the week you lay dying? They'd quote me one price, and then raise the price by fifty-dollars once I explained that you had AIDS. I was so angry with all of these voices over the phone. Joel teased me and asked if I wanted to picket them. I wanted to kill those scared, business-like people. There I was with the Yellow Pages in my lap calling crematoriums while you, my baby brother, lay dying in the hospital. Richie it was so hard. Finally I found the place and it was only half a mile from the hospital, and they were so kind and gentle with me. The woman on the phone told me that all they did now were cremations and funerals for young, gay men; men like you Richie.

I drove there and waited while a man made arrangements for his lover. I sat in the tiny office waiting my turn, sharing the space with a body covered with a sheet, and atop the sheet was a cowboy hat. I know I was in shock because sitting there with that body seemed normal somehow.

When it was my turn to sit at the desk, numbly filling out paperwork, writing a check for your cremation; your cremation, even now the words seem odd, who am I talking about, not you? The woman mentioned that your crystal and gold chain wouldn't melt or burn so the day before you died I removed it from around your neck; I wear it all the time.

SOCKS, CLOTHING AND MISSING YOU

There is a loneliness inside of me that cuts so deeply even buying socks cannot still its persistent, painful presence. I like buying socks. I stand in the store, transfixed by the rainbow of cotton and nylon while images of my clothing flash in my mind. I mix and match the two, the socks, silent on the display wall, neatly, primly displayed. The image of my clothing pushed into the closet, this way, that way. I am not neat. In my mind I wander to my "sock" drawer, it too is in disarray. Just how many pair of pink socks do I own? Do I need more red or blue socks? Is that the right shade of purple to match my new Liz Claiborne sweater? Hmm, how about those socks with stars and moons on them?

Socks used to comfort me. You loved socks, but you loved clothing even more. Your closets were stuffed with clothing. In one closet business suits were neatly hung, in another closet all your casual clothing, shirts, t-shirts, sweaters, Red Reeboks crowded next to classic penny loafers or shiny, tuxedo patent leather slip-ons; and your socks. Not rolled into balls the way I do it but tied together, neatly tied together. So many socks.

Sarah, Helen and I emptied your closets. We didn't know when we would be back to pack up your home and Sarah insisted I start some of the dreaded emptying your home tasks so there would be less to deal with months later.

You remember don't you that Fontelle always said "Richard always smelled sooo good," with an emphasis on the "sooo." I thought about that as I stood in the long, walk-in closet, a small room filled with so many of your things. Your clothing smelled from Polo cologne. I hugged the shirts and suits to me, desperately trying to find you. But all I had in my arms were empty, crumpled pieces of material. Clothing is nothing without a form to fill it and fill it you did; gracefully, handsomely, so dapper in your tuxedo the night of the Emmys in 1982. So casual in your grey sweatshirt and jeans as we strolled through the Beverly Center on a Saturday in L.A.

It is now twenty months since you left. I wear your jackets, the grey, stylish tweedy one that makes me look a bit lost inside of it; after all, Richie, you were 5'9" and I am only 5'2";big sister swimming in baby brother's clothing. Or I wear your black, satin Disney Home Video jacket with Mickey Mouse as the Wizard on the back, gold stars streaming from his wand. I sleep in your t-shirts, especially the one that says, "Mousercise," from the video of the same name that you and your marketing team created. But when it's all too much to bear, this missing you—I wrap myself up in your big, grey sweater and I weep.

JOEL

Time after time Joel flew in from Connecticut to join us in the latest crisis. What awful vigils to share with him. I can see us now; Kevin and me picking Joel up at the airport, the hot Los Angeles sun beating down on us, the choking humidity, and the rotten egg smell stinging our noses from the jet fumes hanging in the brown smoggy air. There's Joel sitting in the front seat weeping into his hands; I am reaching over to touch him, to feel him, to comfort him and myself.

Joel hates hospitals but he was there every time you were admitted with a new health crisis. I think Joel hates hospitals because in nineteen forty-nine, when he was four and half years old, he spent weeks in the lobby and waiting rooms of Bellevue hospital in New York City. I was a one week old infant, dying, on the critical list with a collapsed lung and pneumonia, and the doctors helpless to do anything.

How terrifying it must have been for him, stuck in the lobby of that hospital, scared and alone, while Mom sat by my side, then running downstairs to check with whatever personnel may have been there to keep half an eye on him. Nineteen forty-nine, the dark ages when hospitals had no facilities for siblings of sick babies, and no understanding that mother's needed their well children close by and terrified four year olds needed their mothers. Joel carried that memory in his body and psyche and it was a testimony to his love for you that he was there every single time you were admitted to Sherman Oaks hospital.

Having Joel in Los Angeles dulled some of my fear and blunted some of my loneliness. He didn't even make fun of me when he saw me sleeping with my old stuffed toy, Tiger. Tiger has been with me since I was nine years old. He is fraying everywhere, patched up and sewn all over his once glossy furry body. Joel came in to say goodnight to me, spotting my faithful toy he laughed and said, "Well Richie warned me about Tiger." His smile warmed me in the darkened living room. "Yeah? Good thing he warned you, here he is, funny huh?" But neither one of us laughed. Tiger made me feel safe and for a moment I was a kid again with my big brother saying goodnight.

JOAN ARMATRADING

You loved Joan Armatrading's music. She is singing on the radio, it is June 1991, and I am transported back in time to your car, the staccato rhythms of her music, the soaring velvety notes of her voice floating through the open sunroof as we drove through a hot L.A. Sunday. You really loved her music. Two weeks before you passed away you tried desperately to get tickets to her show in L.A. No one could pull strings; her concert in late July was sold out.

Richie you talked about her long before it was fashionable. Seemed like you were always discovering things before they were trendy. Then you would move on, but not with music. You were loyal to the music you loved; Anita Baker, Randy Crawford, and Esther Phillips. All those sultry voiced amazing women filled your record collection, but above all of them was Joan Armatrading. Joey would tease you and say, "He be loving that stuff. Richie be loving it."

On the one year anniversary of your passing I was in Sonoma with my dear friend Leslie. We dined in an elegant restaurant you would have loved; white tablecloths, fine china and delicious food. After lunch we walked the quiet streets. It was two in the afternoon on a Monday. Leslie and I wandered into a café so she could use their restroom.

As I waited I heard Joan Armatrading's voice singing on the radio that was perched near the hostess' station. It was eerie. I knew and felt that you were with me. I just knew it deep within my heart and soul. The very last time I heard Armatrading's voice was when you lay dying and I held the headset of your Walkman to your ears. I thought it would make you feel better hearing the music you so loved.

The song finished and I walked outside. Leslie emerged and looked at me quizzically. "You look peaceful, did something happen while I was in the restroom?" I told her, "Les, Joan Armatrading was singing on the café's radio just as I was standing there. You know how much Richie loved her music?" Her eyes widened. Leslie understood that there were things in life that were not easily explained by rational thought

She asked me, "Do you think? It had to be. Richie was saying hi to you." I nodded. I was certain that you were reaching out to me from the world beyond the one I lived in. I was unable to speak as tears spilled down my cheeks. Then I remembered Joey's sweet words, "Richie, ahh, Richie be loving her music."

THE NAMES PROJECT QUILT

Autumn 1987

On a cold, dark morning in October I stood along the parameters of the Capitol Mall in Washington D.C. with Alice Wender, Neal Bomberg and their son, Jeremy, who was sitting in a stroller between us. Neal and Alice were good friends of Richie's. Joyce, Sarah's neighbor was with us. It was Joyce and Sarah who had urged me to go to Washington for the unveiling of *The Names Project Quilt*, the ceremony was part of the Gay Right's demonstration being held in our nation's capitol that weekend. Dawn was slowly filling the sky in streaks of pink and grey; my hands, clutching a coffee cup, trembled from the cold and my nervous anticipation.

Morning sunlight bounced off the whiteness of the walkways that lay between the folded squares of cloth. Each square sat like an oversized parachute collapsed in upon itself. The volunteers, clad in white jeans and t-shirts, began unfolding the squares in a silent ballet of bending down, turning around and bending again. Each quilt billowed up and wafted slowly down as the P.A. system began its long litany of names.

Mothers, fathers, lovers, sisters, brothers, friends, volunteers with no personal connection to the quilt, all took their turns reciting the names of the dead. I heard Dan Gardner's name, a friend who passed away in 1984 and James Byron Smith's name, my former boss at Golden Gate University bookstore, where I worked in the early 1980's; Jim passed in December of 1986, two years after his lover, Perry. When I heard Richie's name a sob ripped itself from the depth of my being and my heart broke again. The sound of my sobbing joined the mourning sounds of all those around me; Jeremy began wailing as he saw his mom and dad weeping and holding me in a hug.

I thought back to when my journey here had begun. In March of 1987 I was reading a Bay area newspaper when an article caught my eye. Cleve Jones and Joseph Durant were starting a project to memorialize their many loved ones who had died from AIDS. The project was a vehicle to channel their rage, sorrow, and frustration while creating a beautiful memorial. The quilt would echo the spirit of the times when women came together to visit with friends, alleviate isolation and chronicle their lives. Jones said to the interviewer, "Besides its potential to gain media attention, the project provides a positive means of expressing our community's losses." Durant was one of the first panel makers who'd gotten involved after losing forty friends to the disease. He told the reporter, "by the end of the Christmas holidays I was shell-shocked. I was losing a friend a week. Making these quilts has been cathartic." Durant had created seventeen quilts.

I called the phone number in the article and spoke with Cleve Jones. He was warm and comforting on the phone. "Yes, there's plenty of time to get a quilt in to the project for displaying in the cities you choose as important. I'll mail the directions and measurements, don't hesitate to call with any questions. I'm so sorry about your brother."

Jones told me his larger vision was for the quilt to be brought to Washington D.C. for the Gay Rights march in October over Columbus Day weekend. This was the era of the Regan-Bush White House. During this time the word AIDS was never uttered by anyone in that government. The atmosphere of hatred, fear of AIDS, violence towards anyone with the disease, and increasing anti-gay sentiment was fueled by this indifference as well as the media's predominantly biased reporting on the disease.

It was in this atmosphere that the Quilt was to be displayed in our nation's capitol, in the hope of moving people to search their hearts and souls to find compassion for those with AIDS. Regan and his wife flew out of Washington that day for the holiday weekend at his ranch in Texas. His statement on AIDS rang loud and clear.

Sarah was a gifted seamstress and her creativity always astonished me, whether with sewing, flower arranging, cooking or decorating the house. I couldn't sew beyond putting buttons on a shirt. She asked me to come up with ideas but I was unable to. Then one day she surprised me.

"Hey Suz, come in to the living room, I need to ask you something."

"Sure, let me put the cats down, I'll be right in." I unceremoniously dumped Fred and Zachary to the floor, ignoring their protests, and walked into the living room.

"Sit down on the floor and close your eyes."

"Huh? Okay, what do you have for me, anything tasty, maybe a chocolate cake?'

She laughed, "Just shut up and sit there, and don't peek." Obediently I placed my hands over my closed eyes.

"Okay, you can look now."

A huge paper mock-up of a quilt was spread on the floor. A silhouette of buildings stretched across the paper, each one bearing a name, a synagogue, a video store with a Mickey

Mouse head on it, a building named "Greg's", his favorite bar, the L.A.County Museum of Art, his condo, a gym, a building with the word "mall" on it, a sushi restaurant, *I Love Juicy's*, the macro café he had loved, and a travel agency; running beneath it was a path and under that his name; above all of it, written across a sky scattered with stars, were the words, "When you wish upon a star, makes no difference who you are."

I was overwhelmed with wonder and awe at the sketch of the quilt. She'd taken the essence of his life and distilled it into this work of art. I began to cry. "This is incredible, when did you, how did you?" "I saw you weren't able to come up with anything so I decided to play with some ideas of my own. Do you like it?" "Like it? I love it, you've captured his life, Sarah, this is amazing, inspirational; it's Richie." I reached out and we hugged sitting on the floor in front of her testimony to his life, her gift of love to my brother and me.

Understanding about the deep significance of the quilt dawned in me watching it taking shape under Sarah's creative and loving hands. Here was a marker that said, "Richie lived, this is a bit of who he was, of what the world has lost. Witness and smile, witness and weep."

On the day she finished the quilt we opened the bottle of Dom Perignon Richie had brought back from a trip to Europe in 1984, We had discovered the bottle in his kitchen the week we began packing up his home.

That week I held the quilt, photographed it, pressed it to my chest, and interacted with it as if it were alive. It was alive; it was a tangible memorial to Richie. I didn't want to let it go but I had to let it go because there was a deadline for the quilt to be part of the display in D.C. The quilt was due at the *Names Project* office on Market Street in San Francisco by August; of course it had to be August.

I walked into the *Names Project* headquarters at noon on Monday. Sewing machines lined long tables that were littered with scraps of material, yardsticks, scissors and roll upon roll of quilts waiting to be looked at and grommeted to fit into the finished panels for displaying. Quilts lined the walls and hung from the ceiling, quilts for sons, brothers, uncles, friends, choral groups, quilts for women, quilts for the famous, Rock Hudson and Michael Bennett, quilts for "Anonymous" and "Baby Doe." The quilts bore personal touches, photos, t-shirt scraps, ashes, stuffed toys; each quilt symbolized a human being who had died of AIDS, not a number or statistic, but a living being whose life had touched the lives of those left behind to ache and grieve.

I introduced myself to the woman at the front desk. Her compassionate eyes looked up at mine. "Here's the card for all your information about your quilt. Who is the quilt for?"

"My brother, Richard. My partner created the quilt." I gestured to the workshop, "I feel like I'm in a cemetery, only it's the most colorful, alive cemetery ever."

She nodded, "Yes, it feels very sacred in here and it also feels like home, especially when the workshop is filled with people sewing, laughing, talking, crying; I feel honored to volunteer here."

She was very gentle with me as I filled out the information card. When I finished I reluctantly handed the quilt to her. "We'll take very good care of it Suzanne." I nodded and walked out to the noisy street. I had gone barely ten feet when I collapsed onto the curb sobbing.

So here I now stood on a cold October morning with thousands of other mourners. When the quilts were all laid down we began our slow walk to find Richie's.

Synchronistically we were standing a few feet from the quilt his friend's at Disney Studio had created. Fontelle Slater, Ann Hyatt and Randy Erickson were the designers of the beautiful cloth I was gazing at. Randy had silk-screened photos of Richie right-side up and upside down on a black background with gold glitter and day glo paints scattered across the montage. I stroked the fabric and bent to kiss Richie's face. When I stood up a microphone was near me.

"Hi, my name is Terry Gross and I'm with *All Things Considered* on National Public radio, would you be willing to talk with us and tell us why you're here today in Washington with the quilt?" I was overwhelmed; here was an amazing opportunity to talk about Richie. Before I knew it I was speaking not only about him but about the politics surrounding AIDS.

"I'm here because my brother Richard Fried passed away last year from AIDS, I miss him so very much, and as of today I've also lost six friends to this scourge. I'm also here because it's so important that the nation wake up to this crisis, Ronald Regan and George Bush don't give a damn about AIDS. The hatred towards those with AIDS has to stop. So I guess you can say I'm here to grieve and to make sure Richie and others will be remembered and thought of as real humans and not just as those terrible gay people with AIDS."

Mom told me that the next day, while she was washing the dishes, she heard my interview on her kitchen radio. More strangely orchestrated moments happened that Sunday.

I wandered over to Dan Gardener's quilt, a bright yellow car with a big rainbow had been drawn by my friend Eric's children; Dan and he often had Eric's four children stay at their apartment, as Eric shared custody with his former wife. The children loved Dan and missed him deeply. I sat weeping alongside the quilt when someone tapped me on my shoulder. Looking up I saw a camera leaning towards me and standing next to it was a woman with a microphone. She leaned towards me, "Hi, I'm from the local channel 7 news team and I was wondering if you could talk to us?" I was astounded. In less than a half hour I'd been approached by two media outlets.

"Sure, my name is Suzanne Fried I live in Oakland California."

"Why are you here Suzanne? Is this person related to you?" She gestured at Dan's quilt.

"No, in fact I'm here because there are two quilts for my brother Richie. Dan was a friend." "Would you mind showing us your brother's quilt?" "Not at all, it's over the other way." I led them to Sarah's quilt and knelt in front of it. The camera panned the quilt and the reporter remained silent.

Later that evening Alice, Neal and I watched the local news. I was the only person whose interview was used for the report on the Quilt. What added to the astounding synchronicity of the day was being approached by a newspaper reporter after the television crew left me. The reporter was from San Francisco's afternoon paper, *The Examiner.* When I returned to the west coast I bought a copy of the paper-there was a photo of Richie's quilt and a quote from me. Richie had achieved fame even in death.

After I returned home Sarah teased me about it. "Suz, are you sure you didn't pay those folks to interview you? I know how much you love the spotlight, and Richie sure loved it too." Laughing, I grabbed her into my arms, "Nope, no money exchanged hands but I think Richie pulled strings from above, after all he was great at his job in marketing." As I was falling asleep I nodded to myself. I really felt that Richie, with God's divine intervention, had arranged for the amazing sequence of events that brought his quilt to the public's eyes and ears that day.

In 1988 I received a letter from Cindy Ruskin. She contacted me through the information at the *Names Project* office. She was editing a book for Simon and Schuster and wanted to include Sarah's quilt in the book. Was I willing to have the quilt in the book? Willing? I was ecstatic. I called Sarah. "Sarah, guess what? Richie's quilt, your quilt has been chosen for this book Simon and Schuster are publishing. Can you believe it?"

"Suz, that's incredible, when is it going to be published?" We chatted for a few more minutes and then I hung up. Once again unseen forces were at work ensuring that Richie would be remembered beyond the family and friends who loved him so.

That week I sent Cindy a brief write up about Richie and a few photos of Richie with Joel, with me and one of him hugging his eldest niece, Nicole. Nicole was Joel and Wendy's first child. Richie adored Nicole and she adored her uncle Richie. He tried to see her every time he was on the east coast. Although Nicole was four years old when Richie passed away she felt his loss deeply. The last visit they had was that June in 1986. Tracey, their second child, was one year old, and playing alongside Nicole. I remember Nicole shrieking and giggling in joy as Uncle Richie played dolls with her. Cindy called to ask about the photos I'd sent and I explained the special bond between him and Nicole. "Yes, let's use the photo with Richie and Nicole; it's totally appropriate given their relationship."

Once again I felt God's hand in the attention Richie's quilt attracted.

Sarah's creation had magic and beauty in it; it drew people to it and once they saw it their hearts were forever changed, that quilt glowed with something not of this world.

THE DOOR OPENS

Kicking and screaming I began my journey out of the darkness and into my life without Richie. Life without him was like a quiet hallway with only the sound of one person's footsteps echoing off the walls. Life was like a silent chapel where only the rustle of angel wings could be heard if I listened for them. It was in this void that experiences which could not be dismissed began happening with more frequency.

One evening, a few months after his passing, I was driving across the Richmond-San Rafael bridge sobbing. I'd begun attending a grief support group at the Center for Attitudinal Healing in Sausalito. I hated the long drive home passing the Chevron oil refinery and jockeying through the potholed streets once I crossed the bridge.

The drive unnerved me on top of being so raw from the emotions the group stirred in me.

I began talking aloud, "Richie, why, why did you have to leave me? Why?" I began sobbing harder.

Suddenly the car flooded with the scent of Polo cologne. I was stunned into silence. Then I remembered the golden light in the corner of his hospital room moments after he left his body. Richie was reaching out again to let me know he was with me and that I was truly not alone. My tears stopped and I drove home to Oakland with a sense of peace I hadn't felt in over a year. The next day I called Mom and told her what happened in the car.

"Mom the other night, while I was driving home from my grief group, I was crying and talking to Richie, and Mom, the car flooded with the smell of Polo cologne." She was silent for a moment, and then said, "Sue, I feel Richie all the time when I'm in the kitchen washing dishes. You know that's where he visited with me the most when he came home, sitting in the kitchen with a cup of coffee talking to me about his life while I washed dishes or cooked. Sue? He really is with us isn't he?" Then she began crying softly.

"Mom, yes, he is, I really believe he's visiting us; it's not the same but what an amazing gift it is." Then we were both crying. I knew without a doubt, that Richie wasn't really gone but I still didn't have a framework into which I could place this fragile knowledge.

In the spring of 1991 my skepticism finally fell away. I had a mediumship reading with Hans King, he was just gaining a reputation for his work and a friend had been to see him and was quite impressed with the results of her reading. I made an appointment for his next visit to the Bay area and drove to meet him on a Saturday morning.

I entered the room and sat down across from Hans. He was friendly, funny and warm; nothing approaching my idea of what a medium would be like, which was mysterious, aloof and, well, weird.

"Hello Suzanne, I'm Hans King and I want to welcome you to our time together."

"Hi Hans, I'm happy to be here I've heard some great things about your work." Our reading began with a prayer for protection and then Hans began. "There's a young man in spirit here to say hello. He passed on a few years ago. Do you know who this might be?" "Yes, my brother Richie"

"Well Suzanne, he wants you to know that he visits often and sits on the edge of your bed to say hello." I gasped. Earlier that week I was pulling clothing out of my bedroom closet when I felt Richie's presence so strongly I turned around and looked at the corner of my bed and said, "Richie, is that you here?" Of course silence greeted me; but I just knew it, felt it in my body and my heart that he was with me, sitting in my room hanging out with me.

Hans could not have known this. If I had any skepticism about his work or my experience of Richie in spirit it was immediately dispelled.

Hans continued, "Richie is there helping others with AIDS cross over, and he is surrounded by much music and laughter and light. He says stop worrying you, worry too much. He is fine, it is you that must take care of yourself and move on from your grief."

The reading was a gift, it proved to me that, yes, Richie heard me; no, I wasn't nuts, yes, my mom was also visited by him and that the door between our two worlds was easily opened.

Events took a dramatic turn later that year. I was awake at four a.m., which was a very unusual time for me to be up. I decided to sit at my computer and write in my journal, which had recently replaced my handwritten notebooks.

I was in despair about living alone. Sarah and I had parted ways and once again I was wrestling with loss and grief. I was typing on my keyboard when suddenly words began pouring through my mind and my hands felt as if they were not under my control.

"Just move on and do not worry about things. You worry too much so just relax. I am here with you even if you do not believe what is happening is real. It is time for you to surrender to the God

inside you and not fight it. Let me speak to you, through you. Let your conscious mind go and just flow with me. Let go and do not fear. You are loved by many who are unseen by your eyes. Do not despair. I love you forever and ever Suzie, friend of mine, sister, sweet sister of mine. It is best having you here with me. Know that I am Richard Bruce Fried as you knew me, your baby brother and I am here to say I know it is lonely for you but know that love never dies. Good-bye for now. It is far out sister, Suzanne. I love you so much.. I love your soul. God blesses you. Must go now, back soon, loving you."

I sat stunned staring at my computer screen. Exhausted and overwhelmed I left my desk and crawled into bed. When I awoke hours later my despair had lifted. In my wildest dreams I had never imagined that I would be in communication with Richie ever again.

CONVERSATIONS WITH RICHIE IN SPIRIT

Over and over again Richie visited with me through writing or through my sensing him with me. There will always be skeptics who don't believe the doorway between the two worlds is open and available to all and they are entitled to their viewpoint. I firmly believe that we have lived before, that we have past lifetimes, and that our "job" on the planet is to learn to love ourselves and each other while also acknowledging and experiencing ourselves and every being we share the planet with, as part of the Divine.

I fully embrace the reality that everything is imbued with Divinity and that our work is to wake up to this divinity. Our thoughts, and our negative critic/ego voice, make our lives a heaven or hell on earth. Heaven is not something to aspire to after we pass away and God's "purpose or job" is not to send us to some purgatory or Hell. We create our experiences through how we respond to life; every tragedy has a lesson beneath it and we are either open to the lessons or not. Each lifetime we become more conscious of our inner divinity and the Divine plan for our lives on planet earth.

Living life in the moment is where conscious awareness and God exist. The past is a cancelled check says my guru, Amma. It cannot be brought back and we waste precious energy dwelling on it.

Most of us spend our lives in either the past or future. The time zone of the present is the only place true serenity exists.

Every spiritual teaching, including twelve-step programs, teaches present moment living. My journey through my grief into acceptance and spiritual freedom didn't happen suddenly; it was an arduous process that was gifted with Richie's reaching out to me in spirit. When Richie died my heart shattered and it was through this shattering that my "new life" slowly began.

Over the years my work in the world began changing; and while I still maintain a practice working with adolescents I have a separate practice working as a psychic medium. In 1983 a dear friend, Jan Boddie, who worked as a psychic and healer, trained me to tap into the gifts that I always suspected I had and which I also believed had been passed on to me through my mother.

Mom was extremely psychic and also afraid of her abilities. When Dad was serving in the army during World War II he bought her a Ouija board before he left for his posting. In that war mail was highly censored. Mom received letters with words and sentences cut out by the military censorship office. It is incomprehensible to think of thousands and thousands of letters being censored, by hand, by someone with a scissor, diligently cutting out any references to where the soldier was stationed during the war. Mom asked her Ouija board where Dad was stationed and the reply spelled by the planchette was, "Flour". Three months later Dad's first uncensored letter reached Mom; he was stationed as a medic on a troop ship, the U.S.S. *Pillsbury*. Mom talked about how weird she felt when she used the Ouija board.

"Sue it always felt so strange, like a tingling in my hands, and the planchette moving on its own as I touched it. I finally threw it out, it gave me the creeps, but as you know Dad bought me another one when you kids were teenagers."

I remembered her using the Ouija board when I was fourteen years old. Joel asked what he was going to do when he grew up and the board spelled out "television". Joel excitedly asked, "Doing what?" The reply had my mom giggling before the planchette was done spelling it out, "turning it on and off." We all collapsed in laughter, except Joel, I think he really hoped the Ouija board would tell him about a career in television in some distant future.

Each of us tried putting our fingertips on the planchette with Mom's and I remember feeling how strongly the planchette moved, but Mom always said, "Take your fingers off you're dragging it, it can't work that way." She got rid of the board a few years later. It always gave her the "creeps." There are many schools of thought that say Ouija boards are portals to the other side but usually to malevolent spirits. I for one have never wanted to use a Ouija board, they creeped me out too.

Mom had many psychic experiences of knowing that things would happen or sensing others in spirit; her mother used to take her along before she rented a new apartment for them to live in.

"Grandma always knew I had an ability to sense, to feel that the apartment felt good to move into or if it felt bad to me she trusted that and we would not move in."

I feel sad that my mother did not have a framework to put her amazing abilities into, but I cannot know the path my mother was following for her life; and I am deeply grateful to be heir to some of her gifts.

My conversations, because that's what they are, with Richie in spirit, have been another gift. I share them here in the hope that they will be of comfort to anyone suffering after the loss of a loved one. We truly do not lose each other, when someone leaves their body, or passes on; it is as if they stepped through a doorway to the other side of a reality we, in the body, do not inhabit, but this world is not closed to us.

The nature of reality is far beyond the cultural assumptions. My reality was rocked to its core when Richie began talking to me through my computer keyboard. I hope his words will comfort those who read them as they have comforted me. The first time he used the phrase, "far out" I began to laugh and cry. I had not heard or used that phrase since the 1960's when we were teenagers. It felt like proof, if I needed it, that it was really Richie, my brother talking to me from the other side. His comment on the computer being a "fine machine" startled me; but when I thought about it further I realized that when Richie passed away I was using a manual typewriter and later his IBM Selectric typewriter to write with. Computers were not fixtures in our lives in 1986 as they were becoming in the 1990's.

JANUARY 1994

*S*uzie q, sister of mine, I am happy seeing you. You are surrendering to that power inside yourself, leaping into the unknown, knowing that GOD, the Father, Mother, protects you and that your being in the world is healing for both you and the world. Here I am, linking with your fingers on the key board. Knowing that being here in the words, speaking to me is best, and asking for help and guidance from the angels. They are happy to hear from you and for you to also address them directly.

Goodbye for now. It is far out sister, Suzanne. I love you so much. Let me know when you want to write again. Sure is fine machine for talking to your face. I love your soul. God blesses you too, must go now, back soon. Far out loving you.

FEBRUARY 1994

*H*ere we are sitting in the communication. I know it is hard *for you seeing that Ira is sick now.*(Ira was a friend of Richie's I had connected with in 1986 when Richie visited him and his partner Doug in San Francisco. They had all been friends in the 1970's in New York). *You must say goodbye to him, his body is now torture for him. I know you call to me but know that we are not in the same world and I know how much you miss me. I miss you too but you must know I see your face in the shining light. You think that I am touching your fingers but I am not sure how this works. I am not sad, I may live again in the body someday but for now I live in the spirit.*

Do not be sad for me. Do you think I ever leave your side? I do not dear one.I am there with you knowing your love for me is so strong.

Suzanne, you must not cry over AIDS. AIDS is in the world teaching people about learning to love.

You must practice patience more and more. The world is vaster than you know sister of mine. Forget your anger and your fears. Just love. Let your heart shine in the world. Live your life in the light of God. She holds you so lovingly in Her arms. She is healing your mind and body.

Let the body be a temple. Take care of the body and be healed knowing that God shares in your joy. Let the world see your work and let your face shine in the world.

Don't worry so much. You worry too much about money and your books. There will be many books in your lifetime. Only let the writing flow and do not stop it.

Do not be in despair. We love you so much. To love the world is best in the world of hatred.

Remember the light that holds you. Stars shine and sing your name and the Divine Lord is One. Smiles in your heart make smiles in mine too. So goodbye for now. It is far out sister, Suzanne. Loving you.

FEBRUARY 26, 1994

*S*uzanne! *Happy Birthday to you darling sister of mine. I say to you let go of the past, that we are together in the NOW is best to let that be healing your heartbreak. Making me laugh too, seeing your face the other night at your friend's house.* The biggest love in the room (my friend Frances invited everyone in my closest circle of friends to a beautiful, home—cooked birthday dinner at her home that week). *So many there who love you and unable to say "I love you" but their hearts are so open to your heart, let that be enough. So much love and light, open more to let it in.*

Take on that power you already have, believing in the power of love. Let the leaping come. God holds you in Her loving heart and your fears are but dust. Let the words be unleashed in your heart and soul. You are safe inside and outside, my sister! I am ever by your side. I take your heart and hand in mine and help guide your life to the world.

We are entwined sister, you must believe that you are not alone. I am with you for a long time to come, being here in the astral heaven and inside your heart as you are less afraid to let me in. The brother you lost in the flesh, in the spirit, in the heart, is with you forever. That is the gift from GOD to know me in this way. This is so far out to know you in the way of spirit touching spirit.

Remember that GOD holds us all in loving hands. So let that blessing be. I love you. Knowing you love me. Knowing it forever more. O laughter is so good for your face. Let the heart be glad.

APRIL 1994

*D*ance *in your heart with the light. Let your spirit soar to the skies. How to forget the illusion that the earth is not the happiest place to live? Just know that humans grow through the heart's sadness into joy, forging their way through the night of the soul's darkness. The good inside the heart finds its way. The love you hold inside your heart for one person can light the world. The answers are all inside your hearts. The hearts are the astral connection to the light. Faith means jumping into the void and asking that God holds you as you dive into the light.*

Do not be afraid to ask for your heart's desire, own your passion and your power and stop sitting on it. (Yes, here was Richie in spirit being as forceful about my life as he had been on earth). *Now is the time to burst across the heavens in boldness and brightest blues of cosmic glories. Speak your truth and listen to the answers inside your heart. Angels do hear your words, for the heart is the biggest chapel of light.*

I know that you miss me. I know that your heart is aching, wishing I could be in the body again with you, but I am not being that way for a long time to come.

My hand is not in your hand but in your heart, not being in the way of the flesh. I know that more and more you are liking me in spirit. Your time on earth is for a long time to come. Your mission here is to bring the light. Don't be afraid to push ahead, ask for the doors to open.

I know you hear me in the heart and head. You must believe even more firmly that the separation is not real. It is a mistake to believe

that God is not everywhere, all the time and in your heart and soul.
Good—bye for now darling sister. Doug says hello, he is happy to say
hello to you. Mark is here too. Angels are here too. (Doug passed
on in 1988, before his lover, Ira. Mark Trujillo, Richie's dear
friend who helped us during the six months of Richie's illness,
passed in 1987.)

MAY

*T*his is the best time since we were in the body together, in the Los Angeles city of the snotty angels. Oops, not good to make fun of angels but there it is making you laugh, not sad tonight. You are smiling now, that is good to feel the lightness inside you and the giggles you are famous for.

The world is joyful, not horrible. If you could only see what I see. Many are here to help save the planet. They love them all even those who are as you say, "bad." Indeed it is not that they are bad it is more that they are unknowing of the light within. O sweet Sister, the world is lightness and loving kindness, but that kindness is not the news thing. The news is the worst; it makes you doubt your faith and goodness in all of humanity. That is why it is good to stop watching television. I am here now laughing with you. The joke is that I watched much television when I was in the body. I know now it was not good

Suzie, Hugh is here, Jim, Doug and Mark. Yes, hi Suzie. (At this moment I began thinking of all I did not do when Richie was alive and had AIDS. I felt my guilt about not moving to L.A. and here I was beating myself up again.)

Forgive you? Sister nothing to forgive you for. That is over and you did the best, the best that you could. That is over and you must not hurt yourself anymore. You are here with me to let me know in the body what is on your mind. You must forgive yourself once and for all. I say to you, shouting it to the rooftops, hilltops, and mountains. Let go and be with me as I am now. Your book will sell. The title will be changed to **Loving Richie: The story of the boy and his sister who loved him.**

O now best to wait and do this computer thing. Do it now, do not forget to save the things you write. How incredibly funny this machine is. Lots of new things to learn, that is true, for you to learn, not me. I am not being in the body for a long time to come.

Why did I die? See that no time is the "right time." It is just the time of the dying that comes to each of us differently. In the time of AIDS is the time many of us chose to be here and leave. The broken-hearted way is what happens on the planet. It is losing the many that will save the few that is true.

Believe it Suzie; to be with you in this way is the treat of the century my darling friendsister. Yes, you are always with me that is true and I am with you. Not to fear that we are apart we are not separated by the seeing.

You do not see me? I see you. That is the glow of your being. It is bright and blues and essence and wonderful to see and laugh with you. You are not seeing me? Look over your right shoulder, now in the corner of your eyes. Is that me? Not. Looking is not the way to see me. That is me being silly, sorry of me. Not being mad at me but to look in your heart is the seeing of me.

I always loved you. Love is far out and grand. Slow down and see the love in your life, and the loving, there is so much love that you will be amazed.

JUNE 1994

*Y**ou are asking about the body. It is as you said to your friends; the body is only the shell for the God life force. That is done for you to bring God to the world, in the arts, in music, souls sing much music, just listen to that sound-oooo-it is wonderful to hear that sound! It makes hearts glad to be found in the body. For the time spent here on earth is to be doing the work of God in you. That is why you are all here, not to fear the darkness, it will not win. There is much light being poured into the planet.*

You worry too much. Now you laugh when I say this. So good to hear you laugh. Longing to be on earth is okay so long as you know when you arrive that you are back here to bring love again. So why return to earth when life is so harsh? Life is going to teach more and more that God is inside. The body is a time of forgetting and remembering. Why not remember all the time? This time is when you learn the way to God and HOME. That is nice, letters so big like that!

I am so happy to be visiting with you. Suzieq- you like that I find the "q" key on the computer, you cannot find it for yourself. (This is true; I always have a hard time hitting that key.) *The planet is filled with many who are shining moments of Godlove in their hearts, so lost in the world that they don't know they are Godlove.*

Look, see, that in your heart things are growing so light. Your work is going to shift, a new you is emerging. it is time for you to bring joy to the healing work, just trust the process, trust is the way.

Look for the Mother in the world. See Her in the world; the light you see is Her. YES. She sees the hate in the world. She is sad about the hate. She is trying to heal many. She calls to you and She knows you hear Her call. She is with you all the time. She falters not in Her love for you, and for all. She knows that men and women must learn to love.

Love is so big and there is much love here but people do not know or heed it. People are too preoccupied with money and sex. Sex is okay but not to the exclusion of the loving heart. The body is lovely to see, see that it is the temple that it is, that houses the soul.

AIDS is not punishment. AIDS came here to show that all people need to learn to love themselves and others without judging. This is not punishment, God does not punish. Humans fiercely punish themselves and each other.

For many dying is the way to learn love; for they didn't know they were loved.

So my sister, you ask, did I know that? For many years so happy, then unhappy, so lonely was I. I did not know I was so loved. There were lonely times for me in the city of the angels. So much love there, I saw so little of it I lost my way. So many loved me and let me love them but I was still alone. Yes, my dying was sad. Loved you for being there, so loved you that day.

Good to be here with you again. Just like me seeing you, loving you, is just like good friends, table, dinner. So much to say to you about being up here, that I want to share with you, things to share with the world.

Sister of mine, for a long time I see your sorrow and know the sadness in your heart. Sadness is not good for you. It is good food for you to smile.

Trust the MOTHER. She has the answers. LOVING HER, LOVING YOU. You like that big capital letters thing. See I can do this computer thing, is not so hard. So like my typewriter, my old IBM, you know it! Laughs now, she is laughing, she gave it away to charity, she did soon after I left the body.

Let me know when you want to speak again. From your babybrother, far out, so long for now, see you soon, sweet sister of mine, Suzieq.

AUGUST

*S*uzie, see that the skies are filled with light and you must believe there is that light always in the darkness. Why are children hurt? The globe is crying out with the pain, it is hard to understand all this when you are in the body, so trust is best to have.

So lost was I in the City of Angels. Sister, do not cry for me, to be here with you is the best, know that I did hear you when you spoke to me in the car or wherever you are. I was near and it was good for you to go see that psychic so you knew I was always nearby, especially that day in your room.

How am I not being in the body? I am doing fine. I am wonderful. I listen to music here and I love to dance and I let the light into my life here. Life is so good and sweet and fine; there is music here and in your world too.

I am like an angel and my wings have silken threads to the heart. Did you know that the world is protected by many angels? All people have angels but it is sad that many do not know this, and do not love themselves.

There are many things to do here. Some souls just sleep until they can be alive here in the knowledge of where they are. Some souls waken slowly and even here are not ready to know their true nature.

Do not be lost in the world without me. You are doing fine and it is okay to be alive and do the things you are meant to do. Your lifetime is yours and mine is over now in the flesh, sad to say but true, so let go for now. Know that God takes care of all of us in the body or not in the body.

AIDS is not going to be over for a long time, more people will be dying from it. Do not judge those who do not yet awaken but see your own reflection in their faces without judgment.

You must begin to write that book and do not ever stop writing. Let that work through your mind, heart and fingers and let your ideas out in the world. Let go of that critic that strangles you so.

Now is the time for us to be together in this way. I know you love me, know that I am always in your heart and that nothing separates us ever. Do not weep ever again for missing me. You are in my heart and I am in yours. Good-bye for now sister.

SEPTEMBER

*S*uzanne, *do not be impatient, love all that is before you and see it as your teacher. Leap into the stars and moon above. Practice joy. Go on in your daily living knowing hearts are never parted. When will I be in the world again? Someday but not soon. I am hardly here on the astral plane. I know that eight years seems a long time to you on earth but not being hardly a wink-blink here. I am not able to see your face but in the light hearts glow. It is hard to understand with an earthly mind. Always look inside your heart. Seeing me there with you always. Ira is here asleep. He is not awake. It is not a bad thing, he is a baby soul and Doug is here holding him in his arms and heart. Ira's spirit knows he is safe here.*

I like that you are healing your body more, taking the body for walks and daring to do things from inside your heart and soul. Kindness to your own self must begin at home.

Sister of mine, I must go for I am busy today. Many frightened souls are being asked to cross the river in the heavens, to let their lives go. For now I am providing comfort to many souls dying, and not only from AIDS. Everyone has lifetimes of bringing pain to others and for many lingering longer in their physical pain opens and softens their hearts. O sister, Suzanne Renée, loving you forever. Good-bye for now.

MY WORK

In those years, as my world-view was being stood on its head with contact from Richie, my psychotherapy practice was growing and I found the gift of healing my work was giving, to both my clients and me.

In grief support groups I facilitated, and in individual sessions, clients confided in me their experiences with loved ones in spirit. Clients often asked me if I had experiences similar to their own. I was open with my clients about my experience of Richie in spirit. While I didn't share many details, I would share that, "yes, I have had contact with my loved ones in spirit." They understood that my belief in the realm beyond the earth plane was both a comfort to me as a person and comfortable to me as a clinician.

Some clients didn't even need to ask and assumed that I was open to their experience of contact beyond the seen world; the common denominator was always a sense of relief that they could speak about their experiences and not feel judged, weighed and measured against some cultural norm that was irrelevant to their lives.

I knew how healing it was to feel met and understood by your therapist. Lorraine's journeying with me through those dark times and beyond those early years, was a gift that would always remain in my heart.

My work began evolving into working with adolescents. I sat with children in the social services system who were dealing with multiple losses; fathers, brothers, friends lost to gun violence and the streets of Oakland; impoverished children, losing mothers, sisters, friends, aunties, grandparents to undetected cancer or coronary disease; placement at early ages in group homes and foster care; grief piled upon grief.

I listened to stories of feeling loved ones in spirit urging them not to get into trouble, reaching out to my clients with support and moments of letting them know, as only spirit knows how to do, that even though they were gone from their bodies the love and concern they carried lived on beyond what was seen.

One late summer afternoon a young girl I was working with sat stone-faced across from me. Her beloved grandmother, and the only safe and loving adult in her life, had passed away suddenly from a heart attack. The girl had been referred to me by her school counselor.

"Amelia, can you tell me about your grandmother, what you loved about her?"

Her face softened, opened and then seemed to close off, as if shutters were slammed shut.

"I don't know. I just miss her so much. I hate being alive without her."

"Of course you do."

There was no need for any other words, into the silence her sobbing began. After some time she reached for the Kleenex and blew her nose.

"Amelia, do you want to die?" She shrugged her shoulders, "Dunno, it just hurts, my mom is a total a-hole and she doesn't even want me to talk about Granny. Die? Do I want to die?" She shook her head. "I don't think so but the pain is so awful I don't know what to do."

I nodded, "You're doing what you need to, that's talking with me about your grief, about your granny, and talking to your friends, the ones that you feel can be there for you, working your program, using the tools you have, it's really hard now, but you are doing the best you can."

Amelia, at the age of seventeen, was clean and sober one year from using cocaine and alcohol. Her use had landed her the year before in an inpatient rehab center. Supporting her in staying on track with her sobriety after her grandmother's passing was going to be challenging. "Have you wanted to get high since your granny passed away?"

She nodded. "Have you used?" "No, but I want to." "So what's keeping you from using? She sighed, "Granny was so happy I was clean, she was soo glad I was going to meetings. She still went to *her* twelve step meetings and we'd goof around about her being my sponsor, or me being hers one day. I just kind of feel, well it feels weird to tell you, I haven't told anyone." She stopped talking.

I had been at this crossroad before with clients; I sensed that our working together was about to take a turn into a realm that went beyond the clinical, but was a crucial part of what would be Amelia's ultimate road to healing.

"Amelia, what do you want to tell me? You know your school counselor sent you to me because this is what I do, I work with folks who are dealing with death and dying and whatever comes up for them when someone they loved so very much is gone."

She nodded, sighed, then said very quietly, "I don't want you to think I'm nuts but I feel my granny, sometimes at night, when I'm smashing my face into my pillow so my mom won't hear me crying, I just feel her, there, with me, sort of like she's kneeling by my bedside." She looked at me, checking me out;

was I going to discount what she'd just told me, tell her she was nuts?

"You're not crazy. Many people have that happen after the death of someone they love. Does it scare you when you feel her there?" Astonishment, mingled with relief flooded Amelia's eyes, "No, I feel safe, happy, then I cry even more 'cause she's dead.'" Her sobbing began again.

Over the year we worked together Amelia told me many stories about feeling her beloved grandmother with her. One day a huge monarch butterfly had flown in front of her as she was walking home from school.

"I just know it was Granny, it came out of nowhere and kind of flew around my head, I don't know how I knew it but it really felt like her saying hi to me."

I nodded my head in agreement remembering my own experience the day my friend Jim passed away from AIDS. I was walking down Market Street on my way to the Embarcadero BART station thinking about Jim, I knew he was dying and it was only a matter of days. Our mutual friend, Marcie, had called me the week before to let me know how he was.

My thoughts about Jim were suddenly interrupted when a huge monarch butterfly landed on my chest. Looking down at the creature beating its wings slowly I said "hello". It flew off my coat and when I looked up to follow its path it was gone. Later that evening Marcie called and told me Jim had passed away; it was the exact time the butterfly flew onto my coat.

Amelia struggled enormously with not using drugs or alcohol to numb her pain and managed to get through her first year without a slip back into the endless cycle of her addictive behavior; but we both believed it was in part her grandmother's presence keeping her living her life, one moment at a time on a bad day, and there were many, many bad days. Amelia's grandmother in spirit was a gift to her.

A year later Amelia and I sat in my office for our last session; she was going to college in a month and it was time for us to say goodbye. Her mother had begun her own therapy. Life was not perfect but they were trying to reach out to each other without the rage and blaming I had witnessed when Amelia first came to see me.

"So this is our last session. How are you today?"

She smiled shyly at me. "Good, better than last year at this time." She handed me an envelope. "Don't read it now it's too dorky, mushy, just put it away." She was blushing as she said it. I put the envelope on the table by my side. I looked at her; she had come a long way from the rawness of her early grieving. I would miss our sessions. It was one of the "hazards" of my work, this constant letting go as clients came and went.

"I've been very touched by our time together Amelia, I want you to know I'm always available if you ever need to check in and say hello." She smiled at me.

"Thanks. I'm really excited about going away to college in Boston." We spent the last minutes of the session talking about her living away from home and her excitement of finally leaving high school.

After she left I opened the envelope she had given me. It contained a card with the Serenity Prayer on the outside and inside was a butterfly Amelia had drawn.

AFTERWORD

Richie's words to me are a gift. This book is our gift to you. Yes, I have my days or moments when I seem to forget that I am linked to a greater, vaster love and I have to remind myself that God is walking alongside me; and on difficult days She carries me in Her loving arms. Those days or moments do not last as long as they used to years ago, but I am a work in progress as we all are. There are moments and yes, even days, when I am fully present and I experience life as exhilarating, and the light of all of us stunning in its breathtaking glory.

We are spiritual beings having very human experiences. We are, as I like to say, *Envelopes of God*©; our bodies the vehicles we have been given in this lifetime to manifest the Divine light and love on the planet. Eventually our "envelopes" fall away and the "contents" return to the One who sent us here.

I am here, as we all are, to learn that love is the greatest teacher and gift of all.

It is our work to open our hearts and minds to ourselves and to all our sisters and brothers, easy to say, challenging to live.

In my journey I have been so blessed. The relationship between a sister and brother defies description. It is complex and at times, mystifying. When I speak about Richie people sometimes ask if we were twins. I believe we were twin souls, two Pisces children, swimming along in the crazy currents of life on Earth, a planet filled with massive contradictions. A planet filled with the kind of pain that makes a Pisces wish to escape to the watery depths forever and ignore the world's seeming ugliness. But we shared a deep sense of wanting to bring beauty and light to the world. In his brief time here Richie brought much love and light to those he touched.

Richie is with me always. Your loved ones on the other side are also not far away; we carry each of them in our hearts, as they carry us.

Not the End

RESOURCES

www.amma.org/www.amritapuri.org
Amma, the so-called "hugging saint" was the recipient of the 2002 United Nations Gandhi-King award for Her humanitarian work. Jane Goodall the prior recipient, said of Amma as she handed the award to her at the United Nations in Geneva, "She stands before us, God's love in a human body."

Suzanne Freed may be reached for speaking engagements,psychic mediumship readings and life coaching.
www.envelopesofgod.com
envelopesofgod@yahoo.com

www.birthyourlife.com Bay area California
Body work, psychotherapy, transformative energy psychology. Paula Mcguire.

www.felixleelerma.com
Bay area psychic medium, Felix Lee Lerma.

www.psychic-medium-redding.com
Redding, California psychic medium, Helen Bulthuis.

www.gayprom.org Bay area California
510-247-8200 for information on their annual Clean and Sober Gay Youth and Friends Prom.

www.pflag.org Nationwide support groups and activities for parents and friends of GLBTQ folks.

www.compassionatefriends. Nationwide organization offering support groups, for parents coping with the loss of a child, irregardless of age of the child or reason for their passing.

2069692

Made in the USA